How to Get What You Want

First published in 1999 by
Marino Books
an imprint of Mercier Press
16 Hume Street Dublin 2
Tel: (01) 6615299; Fax: (01) 6618583
E.mail: books@marino.ie

Trade enquiries to CMD Distribution
55A Spruce Avenue
Stillorgan Industrial Park
Blackrock County Dublin
Tel: (01) 294 2556; Fax: (01) 294 2564

© Tom Savage 1999

ISBN 1 86023 082 2

10 9 8 7 6 5 4 3 2 1
A CIP record for this title is available
from the British Library

Cover photo by Moya Nolan
Cover design by Penhouse Design
Printed in Ireland by ColourBooks,
Baldoyle Industrial Estate, Dublin 13

How to Get What You Want

Making Negotiation Work

Tom Savage

To Tess and Anton, who made me a more patient negotiator and a better person

ACKNOWLEDGEMENTS

In reading books, I've always skipped over or only glanced at the acknowledgements. I now wish I hadn't, because I might have learned how to do this right.

There are so many people whose help, support, advice, friendship and understanding have led to the creation of this book that I won't be able to mention them all by name. I am grateful for so much from so many.

The staff in Carr Communications over twenty-five years provided encouragement, inspiration, earthy advice and a happy place to work in. I must thank them: Bunny for first recruiting me; Colette, Frances and Eleanor for enduring me for so long; Brendan and Adrian for forcing me to explain what I thought I knew; Gerard for his understated insight and analysis; Louise for useful clarifying hints; Donal for unfailing good humour and for serving as a literary touchstone and Brona for making me more efficient than I am.

Many friends have long cajoled me to get into print and even provided tips and suggestions. Included are Jackie and Máiread, Máire, Bob, Jim, Margaret; Elizabeth Ann gave precision to an oblique reference; Anne created an authoritative example.

By now thousands of people have participated in seminars and workshops and provided me with challenges, ideas, scenarios and examples; special thanks to my 'adopted' colleagues Dave and Frances. Some like Liam Hogan continue to send key staff members for training; Eileen McDermottroe started the process.

Without the efficiency of Dominique, the manuscript would not have reached the printer until the millennium. Jo O'Donoghue was encouraging, helpful and practical as my editor.

Two people would have wanted to read this book – my departed parents Peter and Mag. I'm still trying to reflect their values and standards.

The most important acknowledgement goes to the Managing Director of Carr Communications (and my wife), Terry Prone. She pushed the idea and the author, read and reread the manuscripts, suggested improvements and, above all, provided unfailing encouragement.

CONTENTS

Contents

1

THE BEST-KEPT SECRET IN COMMUNICATIONS

Negotiation is the best-kept secret in communications.

There are secret negotiators everywhere. Negotiating all day, every day, and keeping it a secret – even from themselves. Negotiation, they believe, is done by a professional minority – and only at work.

Neither of these beliefs is true. Unless you're living in a beehive hut on a one-person island with neither a phone nor a boat at your disposal, you are called on to negotiate with people every day, and several times within each day.

Whether at home, between partners, with children, with your parents, with people who provide services or people with whom you work, the central reality of everyday living is interaction between people. The impact of what you say on somebody else influences the way they see you and act towards you. The way they communicate with you decides your view of what they have to offer you and how you respond to them.

All communication between people is a process of negotiation.

One of the difficulties with negotiation is that people think that it comes naturally to everybody, a bit like listening.

But listening doesn't come naturally to anybody. Most of us can hear. Very few of us know *how to listen*.

The same principle applies to negotiation. Most of us know how to state the results we want. Very few of us know *how to get them*.

Secret negotiators are those who negotiate unbeknownst to themselves, always assume that negotiation is to do with trade unions or politics and believe that the kind of issues that require negotiation skills are high-flown abstruse matters beyond the ken of the rest of us. Not so.

NEGOTIATION IS AN EVERYDAY REALITY

Each one of us is engaged in spoken or unspoken negotiation from the moment we wake up in the morning.

If, for example, there's a baby in the household, the negotiations may start at six in the morning. The baby utters a wake-up call to the world, does some research and makes a statement of need.

Even without words, the message is nonetheless clear to the other people in the house: 'It's morning. I'm awake. Am I alone? Is there anybody else out there? If there is, is that person awake too? I'd like that person to come to me. I'm hungry. I'm really hungry. I want to be held and fed. Or fed and held. Right this minute.'

Now the onus of negotiation shifts to the parents,

who tend to start their negotiation, not with the baby, but with reality: 'Oh, please don't let it be morning. Please, I'm imagining this. Let me get even five more minutes of sleep.'

When you negotiate with reality, reality always wins. So the next phase is negotiation with the baby. Some parents' opening salvo is a series of crooning noises which seek to suggest to the infant that it's not really morning, it just feels like morning, and everybody will have a much better day if the infant goes back to sleep for just a little longer.

Occasionally, this works. Very occasionally. When it doesn't, the negotiation may shift to a negotiation between the parents: 'I got up first yesterday.' 'No you didn't, I've done bottle duty for the past three mornings.' 'Be a star and go a fourth.' 'No.' 'No?' 'No.' 'Oh well.'

For some people, the first negotiation of the day happens in the street, as they engage in the wordless bargaining characteristic of drivers. Take just one example: the driver who has paved over their front garden because they couldn't park on the main road outside their home. There are thousands of those drivers who, every morning, negotiate with total strangers in the stream of traffic that passes on that main road.

By tilted head, questioning glances and meeting or failing to meet someone's eyes, the request to exit on to the road is made, rejected, made and eventually acceded to, the only payoff for the person who accedes to the request an all too occasional raised hand of thanks.

Formal Negotiations at Work

Once we arrive at work, even if our job has nothing to do with industrial relations or trade unions, we are negotiating, verbally or nonverbally, virtually all the time.

- A travel agent may negotiate on the one hand with a client who wants to take her family to Orlando during the autumn half-term break, and on the other hand with an airline which already has all its aircraft booked to the gunwales on those dates, because half the country has had the same bright idea.

- A triage nurse in the Accident and Emergency section of a major hospital will spend her day negotiating with patients suffering from everything from a threatened cardiac arrest to a dislocated little finger, each of whom feels entitled to immediate treatment but many of whom will be forced to wait while the system processes the most acutely ill.

- A publisher may have to negotiate deadlines, print runs and prices with a number of competing printers.

- A student may have to negotiate with another student to borrow lecture notes they missed because of illness, and/or seek from their tutor a relaxation of the deadline on the next essay.

- A homemaker may have to return a microwave that's not working properly.

- An environmental officer within a company may

have to come to an agreement with the Environmental Protection Agency on the phasing out of a particular process judged unfriendly to the environment.

- A new recruit may need to convince her new employer that it would be worth waiting three months for her to arrive, because she'd like to take a holiday as well as give notice to her current employer.

All those interactions are what might be called acknowledged negotiations. Each of the people involved would recognise that what they are doing is negotiating; working on an issue or a problem with a view to an accepted settlement or means of progressing the situation.

UNACKNOWLEDGED NEGOTIATIONS AT WORK
However, in every working day there are also dozens of unacknowledged negotiations:

- The head of administration within a company may bring to the CEO's attention a series of confrontations between heads of different departments as a way of persuading the CEO to insist that all departments use the same computerised scheduling system so that unexpected double-bookings are prevented.
- A secretary may persuade a colleague to proofread a document for her, even though it is not part of that colleague's job, because the secretary dreads the acid comments her boss will make if mistakes

in interpreting her handwriting are not spotted before the document is put in front of her.

- A doctor may persuade a patient that suffering through a heavy cold is a better option than the antibiotics the patient expected to have prescribed for him.
- One worker may persuade another to swap late night shifts because of an imminent family occasion.
- A husband may ring his wife at her place of work and ask her to pick their toddler up from playgroup because he can't get out of an unexpectedly-called meeting.

Effectively, all of those interactions are negotiations. All our communication is designed, ultimately, to get someone to change their behaviour in the interest of somebody else. Pick out any one of those negotiations, either from the acknowledged or the unacknowledged list, and you will realise that, if successfully carried through, not only will the negotiation process achieve the negotiator's objective, it will not leave the other person in the negotiation feeling hard-done-by.

IF NEGOTIATIONS FAIL

Now, imagine that one of those negotiating scenarios was not carried through successfully. At its simplest, this might mean that needs were not met. So:

- The husband might have to ring his mother to ask her to pick up the toddler.
- The publisher might have to increase the cover price

of the book because he failed to achieve the costings he needed.

- The new recruit might have to postpone her trip to the Bahamas.

Those are the simple outcomes of failed negotiations. However, there are usually more complex and subtle results in addition to the simple and obvious. For example, the travel agent may lose business if the customer refuses to accept that all avenues have been tried, or the Accident and Emergency nurse may find fisticuffs breaking out between patients and staff, or worse still, between patient and patient.

The shadow of a failed negotiation is longer than the negotiation itself. In business, where a negotiation is badly managed, a member of staff can end up feeling exploited, coerced, demotivated and disrespected by management. In buying and selling, a customer in a failed negotiation is likely not only to take their business elsewhere, but to do their level best to ensure that, in the words of the old song, they 'never walk alone': they will seek to persuade other customers to go elsewhere also. In private life, the road to relationship break-up is paved with failed negotiations and the air thick with the mutual bitterness and mistrust they engender.

Yet if you ask people to list the skills needed for a successful and happy life, and to put the list in relative priority, negotiation probably won't figure in the list, and it almost certainly won't be up at the top.

LACK OF TRAINING IN NEGOTIATION

For every eighty people who choose to go on Carr Communications presentation skills courses or who are sent on such courses by their companies, only one person attends a negotiation skills course. Why is this the case, if negotiating is such a fundamental day-to-day part of people's family and business life?

Part of the reason is that people see little point in trying to learn the ritual dances they associate with management–union negotiations. (Which is fortunate, because I see no point in them learning that ritual dance either. On a more optimistic note, I do see the faintest glimmerings from some enlightened managers and trade-union negotiators that there must be another way to do business.)

Another reason for the lack of commitment to training in negotiators is an assumption that training can change very little of what people already know and do in their ordinary interactive communications. Over the years in our company we have seen one basic axiom determine whether or not people will opt for training in some aspect of communications. It runs like this:

Human beings will look for help, guidance and training to the extent that they feel their own survival is threatened by not having the requisite skill or not having it in abundance.

Occasionally we ask applicants to communications development programmes to rate themselves on a scale of 1 to 10 on the following communications activities:

(a) One-to-one communications
(b) One-to-one small group communications
(c) One-to-one large group communications
(d) One-to-one local live media communications
(e) One-to-one national live media communications

The self-ascribed ratings usually go something like this:

(a) One-to-one communications
8/9 out of 10
(b) One-to-one small group communications
5/6 out of 10
(c) One-to-one large public group communications
3/4 out of 10
(d) One-to-one local live media communications
2/3 out of 10
(e) One-to-one national live media communications
1 out of 10

Not surprisingly, you will realise from that grouping that if someone is slated to appear on a major TV programme, there is every chance they will beat our door down at almost any cost.

By contrast, negotiation skills tend to be lumped in with the one-to-one communications category in regard to which people feel a high degree of comfort and little threat to personal survival. Until, that is, the individual is given formal responsibility for representing the management of the company in negotiating. Even then they are seldom sent on a training course.

The normal in-company training follows the 'sit-by-

Nellie' approach. Nellie is usually someone already doing the job, but whose actual proficiency has never been tested. It would, of course, be wrong for me to decry the potential of hands-on in-service training. After all, doesn't it work very well in so many areas of skills transfer? Not necessarily so in communications training. You could spend hours, even days, watching the most charismatic presenter at work but be none the wiser as to how the effect was created. Indeed, the likelihood is you would diagnose the wrong causal factor. That's the great irony of trying to learn effective communications skills by watching the great and the good. The better they are at achieving effective outcomes, the harder it is to spot how they do it: the art that conceals art.

When participants arrive at Carr Communications for a negotiation skills course, they are usually conscripts – the worst basis for any programme of learning. Those who are not reluctant tend to be confused as to what precisely they hope to achieve from the experience. Others, while conceding that they are ineffective at negotiating, may be unclear as to where the real deficit in their skill lies.

This book is an attempt at unravelling the myths and mysteries that lie behind negotiations and providing guidelines for the conscripts, the confused and the convinced. The basic message is that getting what you want from negotiations is simple but not easy, always bearing in mind a few lines from the movie *Love Affair*:

The problem is not getting what you want
But wanting it after you get it!

That second line is important. Negotiating is the most common communications activity that we practise at work, at home and in our social life. Most negotiations are ongoing: one leads to another. You must be able to go back. Which means that if you get what you want by verbally beating up the other person, what you end up with may not be what you wanted in the long term.

On the other hand, if you can negotiate successfully and effectively in your more important intimate relations, you are likely to succeed in work negotiations because to be able to conduct unacknowledged negotiations with spouse, partner, children and intimates in ways that are mutually beneficial requires attitudes and approaches that bear fruit in work negotiations.

It is one of the reasons why I believe that women who may have spent considerable time away from work as homemakers undersell themselves to potential employers when they decide to rejoin the salaried workforce. If they reflected on the number of negotiations they would have carried out internally in the home, with suppliers, tradesmen, shopkeepers, travel agents, schools and teachers, doctors and hospitals and others and categorised the learning on their curricula vitae, they would improve their prospects for responsible work positions.

Despite the importance I would place on intimate transactions – enough to merit a book on its own – these pages are focused for the most part on workplace negotiations.

TAKEAWAYS

1 Everybody negotiates every day.
2 Sometimes we negotiate not with words but with signals and body language.
3 At work we engage in formal and acknowledged negotiations.
4 Failed negotiations lead to loss of business, demotivation and relationship break-ups.
5 Not enough people learn the skills of negotiations.
6 It is hard to learn negotiations from role models.
7 Negotiations are simple but not easy.
8 Personal relationships are the best test of our ability to negotiate.

2

COMMUNICATION PATTERNS AT HOME AND IN THE WORKPLACE

Negotiation doesn't happen in a vacuum. Two people don't sit down, free of baggage and context, to do a deal.

Context and baggage are always present. Either can cripple a negotiation. As I was told, during a consultation, by an executive who had recently been head-hunted into a bigger company:

My style of people management is very open. I'm not big into titles and hierarchical structures – I'm happy to roll up my sleeves and help out when there's a crisis. I want to deal with staff in a very direct way and I want them to treat me likewise. For the past few months I've been letting staff and supervisors know that I literally have an open door and I want them to drop in regularly, keep me up to date with what's going on and give me a chance to listen to their ideas about how we can work more effectively together. No one has taken me up on the invitation. What am I doing wrong?

My answer was:

> Probably nothing. The likelihood is that you've moved into a company where the only time a staff member or supervisor entered the manager's room was when they were in trouble for something else. You'll have to start changing the culture.

Within a company like that, negotiations are liable to follow a ritualistic, unproductive pattern. Such a company is not all that exceptional. Over the past few years much of my personal consultancy work has involved carrying out culture and communications audits of multinationals, indigenous large and small companies, health authorities, health boards and state-sponsored organisations. The findings paint a picture of many businesses in which combinations of the following factors exist or predominate:

- Staff believing they are not listened to
- Staff last to be told of changes affecting them
- Staff afraid to talk openly and honestly
- Fear of challenging authority
- Company operates hidden agendas
- Promotions not made on merit
- Inappropriate organisational structures

- Poor communications between management and staff
- Limited opportunities for career development
- Insufficient training
- Staff and management cynicism

NEGATIVE CULTURES CAN VITIATE COMMUNICATIONS

In a business environment where these factors are prevalent, real, principled equitable negotiations suffer. Indeed, I believe it is because of the existence of so many companies and organisations with negative cultures that we need the panoply of mediation and arbitration machinery that operates now. It doesn't have to be so. When trust breaks down, when both sides are not committed to outcomes that are mutually beneficial, third-party outsiders and external structures are needed.

Fortunately, a number of managements and trade unions now realise that there must be a way to do business other than the polemical and antagonistic approaches of the past. One of the most hopeful developments recently was the creation of worker-directors within state-sponsored bodies. They did not initially receive an enthusiastic welcome from all sides. Indeed, in some organisations their arrival led to some managements 'cooking' the communications books. However, worker-directors have been instrumental in changing some cultures very much for the better. A prime example is Bord na Móna. One of their first worker-directors, Mark Nugent, who retired from the post recently, has this to say:

The basic framework that makes negotiation possible is trust. Years of communication and partnership have led to mutual respect and trust. I'm not going to cod you that all is sweetness and light. Sometimes the trust is cut-and-thrust. But the conditions for trust are there:

- A trained and informed workforce
- Informed union representatives
- Management that has been trained in participation
- A culture of partnership
- Worker-directors who take part in all the basic decisions in the company

We as worker-directors have earned the trust of our fellow directors. The external directors look to us to know if a proposal will fly or not and to be guarantors that what management is saying is fair as well as accurate. I am quite sure that if the worker directors were to come out solidly against a proposal, that proposal would *not* be agreed by the board.

This is a major responsibility we carry. We cannot oppose things on principle, we cannot wash our hands of the consequences for the company of anything we say. We must come to the board without any trade union agenda. We can only argue for what is good for the company. Because we have a different perspective, what we think is good for the company may be different from what management thinks. But we are not there to oppose management, rather to bring our wealth of experience and knowledge to inform the board's decisions.

European Legislation will drive the concept of worker involvement in larger companies. But more needs to be done by more companies to create empowerment cultures within which beneficial negotiations can take place as a matter of course rather than by exception.

Of course, it helps if the company is clear on the difference between negotiation and clarification. Some companies don't understand this difference.

You may have a situation where a large company has just completed its strategic plan for the next three years. Its top executives set out to brief the managers in the system about the strategic direction and the implications for themselves, their staff and their customers. The managers believe they are going to help shape the strategy. They're not. It's a fait accompli. Executives chafe at the fact that the managers are not 'buying in' but trying to change aspects of fixed decisions. The managers see the meeting as another example of their not being integrated into a process in which they are key to delivery. Negotiations get a bad name, because

(a there has not been negotiation earlier, when it would have been appropriate and
(b because briefings are now being called 'negotiation'.

My son Anton learned the difference between negotiation and clarification early in life. Normally I try to ensure I'm not working on the Saturday of international rugby matches. The system broke down a few years ago and early on a Saturday morning I asked a sleepy son to video-record the match for me. His response was 'I'll do my best.'

He was rather nonplussed to be greeted with a series of questions:

'Anton, have we a video-tape?'
'Yes.'
'Do you know how to record or programme the machine on automatic?'
'Yes.'
'Then I don't need your best – even your worst will do, as long as I have the match. Is that clear?'
'Yes, Dad.'

I also assume he would have muttered something under his breath. But I saw the match.

Most of us carry into adult negotiation baggage we first packed as children. Parents develop their own patterns of communication which fundamentally shape their children's communicative style. Some families can be described as *accepting*. They teach their children to value harmony, not to show anger, not to challenge their parents or argue with them, and in general not to speak about difficult subjects. Children emerging from such a background find it difficult to take on the other person's perspective.

At the opposite end of the spectrum from *accepting* families are those which can be described as *collaborative*. They believe in the importance of discussions within the family. They encourage children to put across their own point of view even when others may not like it. But they also foster in their offspring an ability to listen to viewpoints with which they may disagree.

In between the *accepting* and the *collaborative* are several mixed categories. What is significant for approaches to negotiation is that whether or not children reflect their parents' point of view, they will almost inevitably replicate their patterns of communication, especially those of the dominant parent.

Many of those learned patterns of communication, if applied to negotiations, will not yield outcomes that are beneficial to both sides. Indeed, it is possible to cluster some of the more frequent approaches which do not create mutually beneficial outcomes into the following categories: the macho approach; the wimp approach; the personality-based approach.

THE MACHO APPROACH

When people with this approach have to negotiate, they summarise their task narrowly and wrongly as: '*How do I get my way?*' over whoever they're negotiating with. Consciously or unconsciously, they just want to find ways to beat other people.

Anyone who has ever played competitive sport knows that there is a great thrill in beating the other guy. None of us has a problem with the athlete who punches the air with delight over a victory. But the negotiator who does the same is very much less acceptable. Not only have they set out to defeat an opponent (rather than achieve an objective) but the victory itself does not sate their appetite for triumphalism. They need the extra kick of talking about it.

The voice of the triumphalist negotiator can be heard in all sorts of locations. Sit at the back of a bus, and you'll hear the accounts of the deadly put-down: 'So, I just said to him, I said . . . ' Read the newspaper profiles of the industrialists who describe themselves as 'tough but fair' and they will be studded with examples. Or buy an autobiography by any of the in-your-face macho managers and one account of victory over the vanquished quickly follows another.

This is where the statement 'I don't do negotiation' may be accurate, because the people I'm talking about are not genuinely interested in negotiation but in getting their own way. Their coat of arms would show them with their foot on the throat of a supine enemy. The thrill of combat is what turns them on and they have little or no care for what other people think or feel or want.

The times they are a-changing, though, and there are fewer contexts these days in which gratuitous bullying is tolerated.

Macho aggressive types in business who simply *bully* other people into doing things feel that they're winning. But it tends to be a short-term victory unless they are in an impregnable position. Eventually they pay the price. This is because, in getting their own way in the short term, they may be losing things that are much more important. Businesses are more successful when management looks beyond deal-winning and sets out to establish long-term relationships. Those long-term relationships can be with customers or suppliers or staff, or all three. The more products and services become like commodities, the more relationship-building emerges as the differentiating factor and the competitive advantage.

Indeed, we're now getting to a point where companies selling large, complex and hugely expensive products or services are laying most emphasis on relationship-building rather than once-off negotiation to a sale, having an advocate on the client's side and nurturing the context for repeat business. That's where good negotiation fits beautifully. Good negotiation? That's where you get what you want by achieving what is reasonable and fair while the other person also recognises an equitable outcome. The door to future progress is left open. Or, as Aristotle put it, 'All that we do is done with an eye to something else.'

The 'macho' approach views the other party as

- an enemy to the vanquished
- an opponent to be beaten
- an adversary to be overcome.

It doesn't end there. The macho negotiator's attitude affects all aspects of the negotiation process through behaviours like:

- Not giving the 'opponent' time to prepare
- Giving a minimum of advance information
- Choosing a venue that suits the aggressor
- Demanding concessions from the outset
- Unsettling the opponent personally in every way
- Reflex distrust of everything proposed
- Digging into your position
- Issuing threats
- Misleading the other side
- Moving towards agreement only if there are one-sided gains
- Concentrating only on the concessions
- Using deadlock as a weapon
- Applying continuous pressure
- Letting the other party know they have lost

Predominantly but not exclusively the macho approach belongs to men.

THE WIMP APPROACH

When people with this approach have to negotiate, they start with a thought process like: 'I hope X is in a good mood. Otherwise I don't think I'll be able to convince them about what I want. As long as I don't sound like a fool . . .'

Here the wimp has totally conceded the initiative to the person on the other side of the table. They have given up hope.

One of the reasons people give up hope long before all is lost is that they have a habit of making cosmic judgements against themselves. A cosmic judgement is where you take one failure and turn it into an unchangeable pattern of personal worthlessness. A smoker, for example, may decide to give up smoking, but cave in after three days of misery. In that situation, some people say to themselves 'Hell, so I failed. I'll have another go next year.' If they do make another attempt to quit the following year, their chances of succeeding are improved, rather than disimproved, by having tried and failed this year. However, the cosmic judgement smokers, as they abandon their resolution and reach for a cigarette, say to themselves, 'I'm useless. I have no self-control. No discipline. I'm never going to get off the fags, I just don't have what it takes.'

Cosmic judgement people tend to interpret comments or feedback as much more negative than they really are. During one recent summer, Carr Communications took on a number of students who wanted experience of our kind of work as well as the opportunity to earn some money during their long summer break. One of them, named Peter, was video-recording an interview I was doing with a client in studio. Peter arrived in studio at the same moment with me and my client and delayed the proceedings while he sorted out tapes, leads and levels. Afterwards, I showed the client into the playback room and went back to the studio.

'Peter,' I said. 'In future I need you to be in studio fifteen minutes before recording time. That way, you're able to check that you have a videotape ready, blank and lined up, that it has the client's name, properly spelled, on the label, that the camera and microphones are working and that there's a carafe of clean water and glasses on the studio table.'

Later that day, when the client had gone, Peter and I were having a cup of tea in the kitchen when he began to laugh quietly.

'My hands should be shaking so much, I shouldn't be able to hold this cup,' he said. 'When you talked to me in studio today, one of the other guys was in the control room and heard what you said. He sympathised with me afterwards over the 'awful rollocking' you'd given me. I was amazed, because I didn't think it was a rollocking at all. Yeah, I could figure from it that I had cocked up on this occasion. But now I know how not to cock up in the future. I don't think you were saying 'Peter, you're garbage, go drown yourself.' Were you?'

I laughed. Whoever had decided that an 'awful rollocking' was what had happened to Peter needed to understand how disabling it is to make such cosmic judgements. Once we make that kind of cosmic judgement against ourselves, we have given up some of our own control, and, in negotiation terms, we have that most dangerous of self-serving salves, an excuse readied in advance.

Excuses readied in advance always have a familiar ring to them, because we have all heard them before. Here's just a sample:

- That job was awarded long before the interviews were scheduled – they were just a cover-up for the

HR guy playing favourites.

- I'm just no good at bullshitting. I tell it like it is and if you don't lick up to management, they reject what you say.
- Well, of course, it's not what you know but who you know.
- It's political pull that gets you those contracts.
- That guy does business on a nudge-nudge, wink-wink basis.
- She's a man's woman, she'd never give the job to another woman.
- They were just going through the motions, putting it out to tender, it's already earmarked for company X.
- There was no point in trying to change his mind, you could tell by his questions he was obsessed by the cost factor.
- Of course there was a hidden agenda there. You know their father had a big row with our first Managing Director?

The wimp approach is founded on an attitude which views the other party as:

- an opponent to be placated
- a colleague to be manipulated
- a friend to be cajoled

It doesn't end there. This attitude feeds into specific behaviours, which affect all aspects of the negotiation process. Wimp negotiators have a tendency to:

- Apologise for wanting the negotiation
- Dither about when and where it should take place
- Agree to any preconditions
- Give concessions from the outset
- Show gratitude for any development
- Vacillate on the issues
- Change their position
- Make offers
- Accept a loss to achieve agreement
- Search for what the other party wants
- Avoid deadlock at all costs
- Give in to minimal pressure
- Say they're happy with the outcome
- Commend the other party for being supportive

I said earlier that the macho approach belonged predominantly to men. More women fall into the wimp category but it also includes a significant number of males.

When the macho and wimp approaches are presented in this way they tend to look like caricatures and the question may be asked: 'Do people really negotiate like that?'

It is a serious question because there is an axiom applicable to human beings which says:

People behave as they do because it works.

It is not too difficult to fathom how the macho approach 'works' – because people see they get their way. But what's the return for the wimp approach?

For those who espouse it, the approach 'works' because they want to be liked, to be seen to value harmony, and do not wish to appear intransigent.

Neither grouping has grasped or has been shown that there is 'another way' to achieve equitable outcomes in human transactions that yields gains to both sides. Before we come to that other way there is one other category I want to touch on.

THE PERSONALITY-BASED APPROACH

Even if people are not simplistically delineated as using either macho or wimp approaches to negotiation they may still have a focus which is at best 'hit or miss' in its application. In other words, in some situations what they do seems to get mutually beneficial results but applied elsewhere it doesn't.

When we create programmes to help people to learn to negotiate more effectively we begin by asking them to list the issues or problems they would like to see dealt with during the training. The issues are among those they have encountered in actual negotiations. A brainstorming session with a group of ten people will come up with a list along the following lines:

- Presenting your case
- Dealing with objections
- Coping with aggressive behaviour
- Handling deadlock
- Achieving compromise
- Coping with emotional responses
- Knowing when to break off

- Handling hidden agendas
- Creating trust
- Dealing with uncooperative people
- Preparing for negotiations

When I looked closely at that listing (and it doesn't tend to vary much from group to group) I came to the following conclusion:

The vast majority of people who engage in negotiations believe that if they had the insight and skills to handle the emotional and personality-based issues that crop up they would negotiate successfully.

Not true. Of course if negotiations break down or are perceived to be unfruitful it is almost inevitable that we will lay the blame on the personality or the approach of the other party. Yet when we videotape re-enactments of real-life negotiations and ask participants on the training programme to assess the process, they come up with quite different causes for success or failure. The tutor will give the group a briefing like this:

'Now that you have viewed the negotiation between Dave and Frances, please write down what you deduced was the real objective of each of them.'

Most of the observers cannot determine the real interests, concerns or needs of either party. Instead they will offer comments like these:

- 'Neither of them seemed to have prepared thoroughly for the encounter, particularly in anticipating the other's concerns.'
- 'There was a lot of talking and little real listening.'
- 'Dave allowed himself to be drawn into unnecessary argument because of personalised comments.'
- 'The agenda kept shifting.'
- 'There was no clarification of what they were agreeing on or even disagreeing on as they went along.'
- 'There were many assertions but little focus on specifics to support the assertions.'
- 'The biggest problem was a lack of clarity.'
- 'At the end they seemed to be in the same position as they were at the beginning, and there are no indications as to how they can resolve it'

Those comments on one individual negotiation could be repeated for 90 per cent of the real-life re-enactments we have videotaped and assessed over the years.

Add to that another curious irony. On the training programmes we do not have both parties to the original negotiation. So one of the other participants is given a short briefing in order to take on the role of the absent negotiator. You might, therefore, assume that the person who 'owns' the negotiation scenario would have little difficulty in achieving a successful outcome when communicating with someone who has only a nodding acquaintance with the details of the case they're representing. That never happens on day one of the training. However, when the negotiator has viewed the first scenario, been helped to analyse the reasons for stalemate or ineffective performance and given a different set of principles and practices to implement, the process of negotiating and the outcomes from a second videotaped exercise are markedly different.

What the participants learn – and it is the main thesis of this book – is that there is an approach to negotiations which is not macho nor wimp nor primarily focused on people or personalities.

TAKEAWAYS

1 Families shape our patterns of communication.
2 Accepting families dull the ability to take on the perspective of another person.
3 Collaborative families foster listening to other viewpoints.
4 Macho negotiators are only interested in getting their way.
5 Wimp negotiators like to be liked.
6 Poor negotiators focus too much on personality issues.
7 There is a way to negotiate which avoids these pitfalls.

3

NEGOTIATIONS ARE ABOUT WISE OUTCOMES

If I represent a big insurance company with a liability, my approach to a claimant is fairly clear: extract the maximum concessions at minimum cost to my company. In that process I use the combinations of carrot and stick, threat and promise that will achieve best value outcome for my firm. I am not in the business of relationships, beyond this one-off transaction. Negotiating is easy, requiring only experience, being comfortable with brinkmanship and a poker-player's ability to calculate the odds against the individual pursuing the claim through the courts.

It is much the same story if I represent one of the big banks and have to deal with a customer who has failed consistently to meet agreed debt repayments. If the bank decides that it wants no long-term relationship with this customer, who represents a chronic bad risk, I can use solicitors' letters or the threat of legal proceedings or repossession of his house to achieve my objective (perhaps taking into account the negative consequences of the public ever finding out my approach).

If I have a worker on a short-term contract with a record of non-performance wanting to negotiate a new contract, I do not need sensitive skills or long training to achieve the desired outcome for my firm: getting rid of that employee.

These are situations where negotiating is easy. On the other hand, where one is in the business of long-term relationships in-company or with external suppliers or customers, negotiating is not easy. Yet there is an approach which is consistent, principled, mutually beneficial and effective. What's more, it is not exclusive to negotiation. In selling, for example, it is relatively easy to obtain one individual piece of business, if that is all you want. But if you want, in addition to the first orders, to have satisfied customers, long-term relationships, repeat business and positive references, then the task is much harder. It becomes strategic selling rather than opportunistic selling.

Strategic negotiating has as its goal a wise outcome, not victory or concession.

It is founded on an attitude which views the other party:

not as an enemy to be vanquished
nor as a friend to be cajoled
but as a colleague involved with you in solving a
shared problem.

It doesn't end there. This attitude feeds into specific behaviours which affect all aspects of the negotiation process, along the following lines:

- Collaborating in setting agendas for negotiation
- Allowing plenty of time for preparation on both sides
- Choosing a venue suitable for the task
- Separating emotions and personalities from the problem to be solved
- Being direct, precise and clear on the issues
- Clarifying and summarising the gains achieved
- Focusing on needs, not positions
- Listening to understand the contribution of the other party
- Developing options for mutual gain
- Allowing space for reflection and (options) generation
- Using objective data in support of proposals
- Changing position in response to principle, not pressure
- Setting dates, measures and milestones for compliance
- Communicating accurately the outcomes achieved

Above I have outlined fourteen possible behaviours which, when combined, will guarantee that you will produce principled, mutually beneficial outcomes from all your negotiations. These may be reduced to the Four Negotiation Imperatives.

THE FOUR NEGOTIATION IMPERATIVES

1 Address issues and problems – not people or emotions.
2 Concentrate on needs, not positions.

3 Develop options for mutual gain.
4 Focus on objective criteria – produce evidence, not assertions.

These are essential. Fail in any one of them and the entire negotiation may fail. If you are very fortunate, the person you encounter on the other side of the negotiation table will set out to achieve the same four, in which case, even if a final agreement is not possible, (because of circumstances outside your control) the negotiation will be positive, efficient and will leave a door open for you to go back at some point in the future.

1 ADDRESS ISSUES AND PROBLEMS
NOT PEOPLE OR EMOTIONS

Human beings find it extraordinarily difficult to separate the viewpoint or behaviour from the man or woman who owns it. The Catholic Church always said that we must hate the sin but love the sinner. It's a good idea that has never had much acceptance: people lump sin and sinner together and hate both with a vengeance.

For example, one flatmate is punctual. The other is not. They have an appointment. The latecomer is late. The punctuality freak turns livid.

'You self-absorbed uncaring swine,' he yells. 'You don't give a toss about anybody else, think only of yourself – '

The punctual flatmate may think this is a way to get the other to change his ways, but as a negotiation opener, it's a dud. There may be some hope of altered behaviour if, on the other hand, the punctual flatmate sits down and establishes the problem:

Fact
They were due to meet at 8.
Action
The friend didn't turn up until 9.20.
Consequence
Because the punctual person had to get some documentation from the latecomer for a meeting later that night, he had to a) wait b) hold up the people at the meeting.
Damage
As a result, the reputation of the punctual one has taken a nosedive with the people at the meeting. Since one of the people delayed is a possible future employer, damage has been done to his employment prospects.
Pattern
This has happened before.
Invitation to collaborate on solution
How can a recurrence be prevented?

As you can see, the second approach carries no blame, nor does it lead to personal attacks which force the latecomer into defend-and-attack. Simplified to its essential parts, this model works – invariably – in this sequence:

- Action
- Consequence
- Invitation to collaborate on solution

So where possible, stick with objective data, concrete consequences and alternative actions rather than emotional reactions.

We try to put this approach into action within our own company, so much so that we now have a little 'corporate phrase' we all quote. We first heard that corporate phrase when a client sent a letter of complaint about a video production we had made for him. The head of video production called in the director of that particular video, who became extremely upset when reading the letter of complaint because the director had, up to then, believed the client to be perfectly happy with the job done.

'I just think this is disgusting,' the director said. 'My feelings are hurt, I feel – '

'Putting your feelings to one side . . . ' responded the head of video production. He was right. In addressing a complaint from a client, you don't start by addressing your outrage or the client's nastiness. You address the issues raised.

Nowadays, whenever someone in our company is getting worked up about something, they'll run into a chorus of 'Putting your feelings to one side . . . '

Of course, the difficulty is that in not becoming *involved* with the other side, you can be perceived as cold and aloof. One of my favourite colleagues is a gentle medic who happens to have a singularly inexpressive face. When people are negotiating with him, they often concede much more than they had intended to because his face gives them the impression that he is implacable and that he will see them dead before he agrees to anything other than total surrender.

He is always astonished when he hears this after a negotiation, but short of taking acting lessons, cannot change the way his face works.

Anyone who knows they have this kind of expression, or that they convey an initial impression of cold toughness, needs to be careful when refusing to be manipulated and when concentrating on issues, not people. They must be wary of inadvertently conveying hostility rather than neutrality.

2   CONCENTRATE ON REAL NEEDS, NOT POSITIONS

Social workers and community development workers sometimes speak of people and communities as having expressed needs, felt needs and real needs. It is not always true that the needs as expressed are the real needs.

Similarly, in negotiations you should not always assume that the positions someone adopts represent the fullness of their needs, concerns or interests. For example, at the beginning of a course, when someone asks me, 'Tom, would you ever close that window?' I might be about to do so, when someone else immediately pipes up and indicates they do not want the window closed.

Now it looks like I'm caught between two conflicting positions: one person wants the window open, one person wants it closed. However, the fact that the individuals' positions are conflicting on the window does not mean that their interests are conflicting.

I might say to one of them, 'Joe, why do you want the window closed?' and he'll say 'Well, I'm sitting directly underneath it.'

'Ah, tell you what,' I'll say, 'How about you change positions – can you pop up here?'

Alternatively, I might ask the other person why she wants the window open, and learn that her interest is in more fresh air, because if the window is closed she believes there isn't enough fresh air in the room.

Once I have worked out her interest, then I can say, 'Would it be OK if I opened the door or turned up the air conditioning?'

So what initially presents as diametrically opposed positions are two interests which are not mutually exclusive at all. This happens in all negotiations.

A guy with a debt may say, 'I'm not paying.' That's his position. Now his interest is that he doesn't want a debt hanging over this head. But he's struggling. This allows the negotiator to say: 'You're prepared to pay it back, but you're under pressure. So we've already agreed that you owe the money, but you'd like it phased out over a longer period so that you're not under such pressure. Now, when it comes to the period of time, what do you think is reasonable?'

Addressing interests rather than positions is not going soft. Having identified the debtor's interest, you can ask, 'Why is that all you can offer? What other commitments do you have?' So you're exploring around your collective interests. Your objective, obviously, is to get paid. His interest is to get rid of the debt. What you are trying to do is to create options for both sides and because you are talking interests, rather than holding to positions, like two people painted into the opposite corners of a room, the process is under way, the dynamic of negotiation is actually working.

Interests are about needs, fears, concerns. They motivate you to want something and to give something. Here are two stories, one of which illustrates the tragic outcomes of not understanding and expressing real interests, while the other shows how relationships can be sustained and developed despite differences in positions once the concentration is on real interests.

Not in this family
A family is living in the south of Ireland – father, mother and four children. The eldest boy is married with a young family. The second son is single, aged twenty-seven – let's call him Derek. The others, a boy and a girl, are attending university.

Derek has become involved with a woman who has two children and is separated from her husband. When the parents hear of the relationship, they are upset and furious with Derek – and say so. He ignores their intervention and comments and later moves in to live with his new partner.

Shortly afterwards, he pays a visit to the family home and there is a knock-down drag-out family row. Accusations are flung from both sides at both sides. Very strong negative statements are made, such as:

- 'You don't care about your parents and family – you're only interested in your own selfish needs.'
- 'All you two care about is what the neighbours are saying – you don't care a toss about me.'

The language, the emotion and the heat escalate. Derek storms out to a chorus of: 'We don't want any more of *that* – not in this family.'

He goes to the local bar. Gets drunk. At 11.45 pm, he sets out to drive home, loses control of the car, crashes into an electricity pole and is killed.

The parents will probably never have a happy day again. They feel, wrongly, that they were responsible for his death. They wish they could rerun that evening, that process of communication and negotiation.

Their real fear and concerns were:

- the unresolved situation between the woman and her husband and Derek's role in the middle of it
- whether or not Derek could support an already existing family on his meagre salary
- that his own growth and development might be hindered by the relationship
- whether they could have fruitful communication with the new person in his life

Did they think out and express any of these real interests and concerns? No. Many of the real tragedies of Irish family life happen because people take up positions when they should be looking at interests.

They loved him and wanted him to be happy. Did they tell him so? No. And Peter died.

Denver and parents

After John Denver's death, an American radio station broadcast an interview in which the singer told of how he rang his parents to announce that he was quitting his studies, six months before finals, to follow a singing career. At that time, his father was recently retired and his family was not very well off.

A few days after giving the news to his parents, Denver received a letter from his father which had sentiments something like this:

'Your mother and I are very disappointed that you did not complete your studies. You know how precarious a musical career is and we feel you should have had a qualification to fall back on.

'However – you've made your decision. In the next few months, you're going to be short of money, so enclosed is a cheque to keep you going. You know how much we both love you and we look forward to seeing you if you're near home.'

This is a classic representation of how two sides differed in positions (on the study issue) but communicated openly about their real interests (the ongoing relationship). In that lay the potential for mutual gain at that moment or in the future.

John Denver's own comment was that he never forgot the letter or its implications and that it changed his life.

Whether the object of negotiation is family happiness,

industrial harmony or the survival of a government, this distinction between interests and positions can never be made too clearly.

Case study: addressing issues, not positions
In the summer of 1994, there was a lot of tension at government level in Ireland about the impending appointment of Attorney General Harry Whelehan as President of the High Court. The topic was constantly in the papers, and a good deal of position-taking was going on around it. As Tánaiste, Dick Spring's attitude was hardening, and in direct response, Albert Reynolds, Taoiseach at the time, was becoming more entrenched in his position, determined to 'deliver' the appointment.

I was Special Adviser to the Taoiseach, but had kept out of what I saw as an issue neither of communication nor policy. Eventually, two members of the Cabinet said to me: 'Look, you'll have to talk to this man and get him to see sense. Yes, he can, if he wants to, rub Dick Spring's nose in it and use a majority at Cabinet to push this Whelehan decision through – in which case he'll create more problems than he's experienced up to now.'

So I sat down with the Taoiseach, who was fulminating about the Labour Leader and his advisers and what he saw as their manipulation of media. In this context, his delivery of the appointment of Harry Whelehan amounted to an assertion of his leadership.

'OK,' I said. 'You can certainly do that. You have the power. But let's just for a moment figure out what is it that you want – '

'I want this appointment,' he said. 'I want the whole thing done and out of the way.'

'Fine,' I said. 'That's the short term.'

'What do you mean?'

'Well, I presume you want this government to complete its term?'

'Yeah.'

'I presume that, whether publicly or privately, you want an understanding built, coming up to the next general election, that despite having a reputation as being difficult to work with, you're not, and that there's a tacit – or even an explicit – understanding that Fianna Fáil and Labour will enter the election planning to form another coalition government afterwards. You want that because all that you're committed to, especially peace in the North, can't be achieved in the next two years but needs another term. And you want to establish yourself as a statesman and one of the finest leaders of your party. Is that what you want?'

'Yes.'

'Right. If that's what you want, long term, then if, in the short term, you just force this thing through against the will of the Labour Party, it doesn't take a rocket scientist to predict that what's going to happen is that within the next five months, they are going to walk out. And they're going to walk out having made very sure in the interim that you're seen as being to blame for the breakdown. All the really important things you want to happen can't then happen, because they won't go into an election as partners and you won't be able to get any other party to coalesce with you. Now, if you want to prevent that happening, you have to sit down with Dick Spring and his people – and your own front bench – and look, not just at the Whelehan issue, but at the longer term. You have to listen to their concerns about other banana skins they believe are just around the corner waiting to wreck this government – listen openly. I suspect the only way to do it is to take the Cabinet away somewhere quiet, secluded, where in a different context tensions can cool down, understandings can be reached and a new framework put around this government.'

'I'll do it,' he said.

Very shortly afterwards, it was announced that the Cabinet was going away for discussions in Tinakilly House, and when both elements of the Coalition emerged from the building afterwards the calm and good humour were almost palpable. The Cabinet ministers who had originally asked me to get involved both rang me, thrilled with what had been achieved, proud of the Taoiseach and confident of a full term in office, followed by re-election in partnership with Labour.

The fact that the agreement didn't last and that relationships were sundered relates to another element in negotiation – protecting the agreement – that will be dealt with later.

It is vital for effective negotiations that both sides have the ability to work out their own real needs and those of the other party. However, many people enter into negotiations without ever reflecting on what even their own real interests are.

They find it difficult not just to express their needs and interests but to formulate them in any conscious sense. Yet one of the other key imperatives in successful negotiation – developing options for mutual gain – depends crucially on the capacities of the participants to know and express their real concerns.

3 DEVELOP OPTIONS FOR MUTUAL GAIN

Once you have a good understanding of the real needs, concerns or interests of the other party you can begin to envisage a range of options to meet those needs. In the earlier simple example of someone wanting a window open, it was possible to suggest:

- a change of position
- opening of a door
- lowering the temperature

as some of the options, in order to meet the real needs of the individuals.

Recently, a friend of mine was being headhunted by a large private company from her safe, secure, pensionable job in a state-sponsored body. She was being offered a higher salary, but that was not her prime concern. Instead, she was concerned about the reputation her new managing director had for being capricious and volatile, and she was wondering how the extra travel would affect her time for her young daughter. Based on these real needs, she was able to discuss various options like:

- additional contributions to her pension
- flexi-start and finish times as required
- maximum annual leave
- objective criteria for performance reviews

All these were acceptable to her new employer, who was delighted with the appointment.

Here again you can see how knowledge of real needs can help both sides to agree to options for mutual gain. This has been worked out in a full case-study at the end of this chapter showing all four imperatives in operation.

It is important that both sides think about options for gain before coming to the negotiation. But they should not forget that they are colleagues looking for solutions to shared problems so they can brainstorm together during the negotiations knowing that such synergy will generate more options than individuals could do by themselves. That will also have the benefit of more ready ownership of the options thus created.

4   Focus on Objective Criteria –
Produce Evidence, not Assertions

Recently a woman came to me to discuss an upcoming negotiation.

She was formerly the marketing manager of the Irish subsidiary of a Europe-wide company. Four months before our meeting the managing director of the Irish operation had been fired for being ineffective and she had been asked by the parent company to serve as acting managing director. She took on the post on a temporary basis but now the executive to whom she reported wanted to discuss the terms and conditions under which she would agree to take on the post permanently.

This was her dilemma. In her post as marketing manager she had a salary of £35,000 per annum, with a contribution being made by her employers to her pension, plus travelling expenses on an agreed rate for visiting the twenty branches of the organisation. At the time of his firing the managing director was on a salary of £50,000 plus the usual company car and pension contributions. Her comment to me was:

> It's not as if I am an outsider coming in to take over the job. They know that I am on a salary of £35,000 and there's no way they're going to offer me anything like £50,000 to carry on in the job. Yet that's what they were paying to someone who was totally ineffective over a number of years. I'm reluctant to take on the same job, requiring a huge effort to rectify the mistakes of the last managing director for a figure substantially below what he was getting.

Her observations were realistic. The executive with whom she was to negotiate was probably going to offer something like £5,000 more than she was currently earning as an inducement for her to take the job permanently. And he would have been fairly confident that she would agree because it was a significant improvement on her present position, plus she would now get a company car. In addition she liked the company, was effective in her job and would be unlikely to throw away the opportunity to continue to be the boss.

The first suggestion I made to her was to postpone the negotiation for at least ten days. (It was due two days after our meeting.) In the intervening period she was to:

- obtain information on salary levels for managing directors of equivalent operations in Ireland
- find out the going rate for managing directors of the British and European subsidiaries or the regional managers (whatever was similar in branches and employee numbers to the company in Ireland)
- collate all the figures on turnover and net profitability since she had assumed the role of managing director (there had been significant improvements)
- document the effect of changes she had introduced in inventory control through computerisation
- decide on the percentage level of contribution she wanted for her pension
- outline on paper the non-financial, non-statistical changes she had introduced to improve the efficiency of the company
- write down her targets short-term, medium- and long-term, based on current performance

Armed with all that objective data she was to approach the negotiation aiming at a salary figure in the region of £45,000 but including a clause that her salary would be subject to review after six months in line with productivity changes in the Irish subsidiary.

She was successful in her negotiation.

What were the other approaches she could have adopted?

She could have made a number of unsubstantiated claims about how well she was doing: 'Things are great since I took over; the staff are very happy.'

She could have allowed her negotiations to be peppered with assertions like: 'I think I deserve more than that' or 'You should pay me the same as you paid the former managing director' or 'That's not fair.'

She could have whinged a lot: 'You're only doing this because I am a woman.' 'I feel totally demotivated at the way I am being treated.'

She could have threatened: 'I will have to consider my position within the company.' 'Wait till the staff hear about how I am being treated.'

She could have lied: 'I have been approached by another company with a high salary offer.'

She could simply have accepted whatever the company executive offered.

None of those approaches would have yielded an outcome that was equitable, mutually satisfactory and reinforcing of the relationship between employer and employee for the future. In real negotiations you do not use threats or pleas. Instead you insist on using objective criteria and create movement based on the power of the evidence.

Case study: Negotiation Imperatives at Work

Potential Employee
Position
Would like a new job, more money (present salary £36,000) plus pension contribution, plus travelling expenses

Interest or Concerns
Needs private-sector experience

No career development possibilities in present job

MD has reputation for being capricious and volatile

Further to travel

Longer away from little daughter

Managing Director
Position
Needs replacement for departed executive, not to exceed salary cap of £36,000; pension contributions, travelling expenses

Interest or Concerns
High turnover in post over past three years

Needs person with internal as well as external communications skills

Knows this woman has strong family commitments

She has moved regularly within state-sponsored sector

Separate people from issues

Not a Script Like This

A: 'I believe you're a rather capricious MD, who can be difficult to work with.

B 'You're not exactly a settled person yourself. You have been all over the place in the last few years. Anyway are you the sort of person who listens to rumour and gossip from inside companies?'

A 'Of course not! But there have been a lot of people in this job recently and I wonder why they've all left.'

B 'Would you like to hear the reasons or have you already made your mind up?'

(We know where this negotiation is going.)

What are the issues?

- Focus on objective criteria
- Clarity of the specification of the job
- Establishing targets
- Monitoring and reporting on performance
- The salary cap vis-à-vis current income
- Home concerns

Options for mutual gain

On Salary

Provision of laptop computer and modem for more working from home (family interests being preserved)

Higher contributions to pension

Early morning customer meetings near home so

that additional travel expenses are possible
On Home Concerns
More remote working and flexitime
Maximum holiday leave
Time off in lieu of evening working
On volatility or frequent moving
Commitment to clear job specifications
Performance review based on performance agree-
ment
Salary review based on performance

TAKEAWAYS

1 When continuing relationships are of no account, negotiating is easy.

2 If you value long-term relationships, you take a strategic approach to negotiations.

3 Both parties in negotiations are colleagues involved in solving shared problems.

4 Address behaviours and issues, not people and emotions.

5 Concentrate on needs, not positions.

6 Develop options for mutual gain.

7 Prepare and use objective criteria – no emotional reflexes or unplanned scripts.

8 Use evidence, not assertions.

4

Negotiating with a Company New to You

For the most part you will find yourself negotiating with individuals or organisations you already know quite a lot about. This does not absolve you from the responsibility to carry out focused preparation for the specific negotiation. However, quite often the individuals and the company they represent will be new to you. This demands very thorough advance research, exploratory meetings and sifting of what you have gleaned. Your overarching aim is to establish what makes this company special and different and what are the needs, interests or concerns that will shape the negotiation with you.

Read the Published Material
Start with any published information you can find about the company or organisation. Annual reports provide basic factual, statistical and financial information. They seldom yield any real insights into whatever truly differentiates the organisation, unless the chairperson or chief executive has an input into the reports.

Some do. Mostly the task devolves to the head of public affairs or other internal or external consultants. Occasionally, though, you will find something written from the heart by one of the key figures within a company, and this, carefully read, can be enormously powerful in its revelation of the corporate or individual mindset. Look up what's stated about the firm in the company's office. Check newspaper files to see what has been reported on over the past few years. Find out if the organisation has a website and read what is on offer. I have no doubt that the Internet is going to be the prime source of information about businesses in the future (and the future is now).

Recently in Carr Communications we were providing a training programme for a political party. One of the tutors/trainers had never met the politicians before and many of them were backbenchers or senators without a significant national profile. Yet she was able to greet them by name, knew details of their qualifications and careers and was able to astound one of them by saying, 'You are now living in the house that was previously owned by my parents' best friends.' All this had been discovered from intelligent reading of the website of the political party, which was informative and carried pictures of the individuals and other relevant data.

Written information is not usually the best source for providing insight, but perceptive analysis even of sparse material can yield unexpected returns.

Here's an example we have used to improve trainers' uptake from written material.

First of all we give this brief: What you're about to read was written by one of the major leaders of the twentieth century. Can you figure out from the content who it was?'

Then we provide this text:

Let us imagine the following: In a basement apartment of two stuffy rooms live a worker's family. . . Among the five children there is a boy, let us say, of three. This is the age at which a child becomes conscious of his first impressions. In gifted people, traces of these early memories are found even in old age. The smallness and overcrowding of the rooms do not create favourable conditions. Quarrelling and nagging often arise because of this. In such circumstances people do not 'so much' live with one another, [as] push down on one another. Every argument . . . leads to a never-ending disgusting quarrel . . .

But when the parents fight almost daily, their brutality leaves nothing to the imagination: then the results of such visual education must slowly but inevitably become apparent in the little ones – especially when the mutual difficulties express themselves in the form of brutal attacks on the part of the father towards the mother or assaults due to drunkenness. The poor little boy at the age of six, senses things which would make even a grown-up shudder. Morally infected . . . the young 'citizen' wanders off to become one of the dangerous disaffected members of society.

All sorts of answers emerge. Someone, looking at the references to poverty and overcrowding, may speculate that it might be Roosevelt of the New Deal. Someone else may think of Lyndon Johnson and his War on Poverty. Others will look to early British Labour Party leaders. One recent reader, however, responded with this written analysis:

This looks like it has been dodgily translated by an American. The words 'workers' and 'citizen' look a little socialist – maybe Stalin. The thinking is tortuous – an ill-conceived hypothetical situation designed purely to support the writer's thoughts – and seems to be aimed at singling out a grouping for harsh treatment. Stalin is still strongly in the running but I would be tempted to add Hitler.

Lastly there is the fact that whoever wrote this doesn't seem to like the people he's talking about at all. (Hitler hated his own family so he seems more likely.) He also has intellectual pretensions (that stuff about impressions in three-year-olds).

Also you said 'great leader of the twentieth century.' Could there have been an element of sarcasm there?

So we're looking for an elitist, non-English speaking, pseudo-intellectual with a nasty agenda he can't back up with reality.

Hitler or one of the other fascist leaders would seem the most likely candidate.

The reader was correct – Hitler was the writer.

That's the kind of observant, sceptical (not cynical) eye that needs to be brought to bear on any written material coming from an individual or company with whom, in the future, negotiations are planned.

TALK TO PEOPLE WHO KNOW THE COMPANY

When you're setting out to discover what differentiates a company from all others, some facts will pop up quickly, especially if the company has a publicised company legend. Most people know, for example, that Apple was started by two guys working in a garage, that Dell computer was started by an extraordinarily young entrepreneur, and that Intel has a culture of 'constructive confrontation' emanating directly from Bob Noyce.

That's the first layer of differentiation. The second layer is usually easy to explore without the need for any microscope or searching questions. Two examples.

1 When Hewlett Packard set up in Ireland, before they even moved into their premises, they got up and running in a temporary place on the northside of Dublin. They hired my company to do a training course for them. Two of our executives arrived. One of them, notorious back then for his commitment to being a slob, looked

around him as he set up the cameras and observed, with astonishment, 'Hey, I'm overdressed here. I'm too neat!' He was right. This corporation is determinedly casual in its non-dress code, so even a somewhat rumpled suit stood out.

2 Working with an environmental committee related to the chemical industry, our executive was amused to hear one of the participants putting on a prissy voice and saying 'We in Eli Lilly . . . ' When she sought clarification it emerged that whenever Lilly executives attended committee meetings, they were notable for their straightforward belief that, whatever about the others, they and their company were leaders in environmental responsibility. They all had a sense of belonging to the best.

Now, neither of those bits of information are what you pick up from an annual report. They are, nonetheless, extremely valuable, were you to find yourself in a negotiating position with either company. At its simplest, you are likely to do better with Hewlett Packard if you don't go to talk to them in formal dress, and you are likely to do better with Eli Lilly if you don't lump them in with companies that do not have their standards or *esprit de corps*.

HOLD INSIGHT-FINDING MEETINGS

(Note that the word I've used is not 'fact-finding' but 'insight-finding'.)

In many selling, negotiating or pitching-for-business

situations, it is appropriate, even routine, to seek an opportunity to interview the people with whom you will subsequently be communicating. In fact, these days, corporations will often put a black mark against you if you fail to go through this preparatory research phase because they assume you don't care enough to learn about them and are just going to make the same pitch to them as you might make to any one of a hundred other companies.

The exploratory visit is now a 'given' for many service organisations. And pretty damn fruitless it is too more often than not.

This was illustrated by a management consultancy group with which I recently worked. One of the senior management guys indicated that as well as the folders of data, they had extra research. Two of them had gone to the prospective client's premises to do in-depth personal, on-the-spot investigation.

'What did you find out?' I asked.

They told me that the company was looking for consultancy on X and Y (they knew that from the letter inviting proposals), that the company made Z for the W market (that's all in background material. They didn't need a visit to find out about it) and that the consultancy that's had the account up to now was pitching to retain it. (Not new – available on the grapevine.)

Added value? None. Any personal observations? Not really. How long did the visit take? Fifty minutes. How long had been allocated by the client – or prospective client – for it? One hour. So not all of the time had been used? Well, there's just so much we felt we could say about our service – we explained how long we've been in business, and how many we employ and what our turnover is.

'Lads,' I said. 'As management consultants, you may be geniuses, but as researchers, you're not at the starting blocks.'

Tips for Insight-finding Meetings

1   *Have them on premises of the company with which you are about to negotiate and learn from its environment.*

Your eyes can pick up enormous amounts of information for you, and they should start doing that long before you enter the offices of the person who has agreed to see you. The car park of any large company or organisation speaks volumes about that entity. It will tell you, by the way it is laid out and by the way its spaces are designated, how hierarchical is the body, how committed to diversity and how interested in customer care.

The signage is another clue. Does it start from where the neophyte is at, or is it a reflection of what the organisation itself thinks important? The displays in the lobby are also important, as are the attitude and response of the staff in lobbies and corridors. My company some years back decided not to market to one large successful manufacturer, because the atmosphere of fear and of pressure within the company's HQ and branches was palpable. If you walked down one of the corridors with one of their top management, for instance, any staff member coming in the opposite direction instinctively dropped their gaze and moved faster. Contrast that with companies where meetings in corridors spark off warm smiles, greetings by first name, exchanges of mock abuse, and you have a significant clue to the reality of the different corporate cultures exemplified.

2 Create a positive atmosphere

The first thing that happens in most negotiations is introductions, which require a warm firm handshake and exchange of names.

Older even than 'the cheque is in the post' is the excuse that 'I've an awful head for names.' I have never accepted that excuse. Remembering names is not a function of genetic endowment. It is an end result of paying attention to someone other than yourself.

At a party, for instance, when the new arrival is introduced to five people already standing around clutching their drinks, the new arrival smiles, shakes hands, accepts a drink – and, if they're honest, would confess that even three minutes after the introductions, they can remember not one of the names. The reason is that new arrivals at a party are self-conscious, perhaps even nervous. Going through their head is a litany: 'God, I won't know anybody here, I wonder have I picked the right kind of outfit, hope someone has a drink lined up for me, Lord, that guy looks familiar, who the hell is he, this is a very glamorous woman, I hope that's not curry I smell from the kitchen.' They are, in short, concerned with their own needs and feelings, so the transmission of the names of other guests is blocked at point of entry.

On the other hand, the arriving guest who makes an effort to make other people comfortable will concentrate as the handshakes happen, will make sure they pick up the names, and will use them quickly.

'Marie – let me get it right, is it Marie or Mar*ie*?'

'Sorry, I didn't hear your name over the laughter, what was it again? David? Thank you, David.'

Using names reinforces them in our minds. Overusing names makes us sound like archetypal used-car sellers.

All that is required is attention. No magical memory. So convinced have I always been of the importance of learning names – I'll come back to why it's important in just a minute – that, as head of training in the company, I have banned lapel-badges and nameplates on tables. Each one of our tutors must start a course, which may have twelve, or in rare cases, fourteen participants, without a list of names in front of the tutor and without nameplates in front of the trainees, and by the first coffee break, must be absolutely *au fait* with each and every name around the room. In the beginning, tutors are scared by our insistence on their learning names. Within weeks, they have joined the ranks of the convinced, and take some pride, as we all do, in the absence of nameplates. We cannot imagine anything less likely to make people feel warmly appreciated than to have someone fail to meet their eyes because they need to look at their name on a desk or their name-badge on the right side of their chest.

I became aware of the importance to each individual of their name, particularly their first name, when I was doing a lot of work in hospitals. I noticed, in intensive care units, that the nurses spent a good deal of their time literally shouting at the patients in ICU, trying to rouse them from coma or reach them through anaesthetics. The shouts always began with the patient's first name, because, as one nurse bluntly told me, 'Our names are the first thing we really respond to in life – and they're the last thing. Once someone terminally ill has stopped responding to their own name, their dying is just a matter of time . . .

Names are important. Demonstrating the courtesy, attention and respect for the individual implicit in getting their name right – and keeping it right – can make a substantive contribution to the creation of a positive atmosphere in any serious negotiation.

John Cleese has said that you don't have to be sombre in order to be serious. My own chairman, Bunny Carr, has always said that you can be grave without being funereal.

The best example I have come across of someone creating a positive atmosphere even in a life-or-death situation was demonstrated by, of all things, a black box flight recorder. This is the device which comes into play after a plane crash, when the recordings it has captured of flight-deck conversations can give accident investigators useful clues as to what happened. The device itself is virtually indestructible.

The recording I have in mind came to public attention as a result of a crash in 1989 in Sioux City, Iowa, in which almost a third of the passengers and crew on board died. What happened was that debris from an in-flight explosion in an engine cut the hydraulics on the plane, so the pilot, Al Haynes, who was pushing sixty years of age, had no steering mechanism at his disposal, although he managed, by using the throttles of the two functional engines, to manoeuvre the plane a bit. For more than forty minutes, Haynes negotiated with ground control, with his own crew and with a pilot who happened to be travelling on the plane as a passenger, to achieve the best crash-landing possible. What is startling, if you read the transcript of that negotiation, is the good humour Haynes maintains – while staying in focus – and how it infects the rest of the people.

The crew try option after option, and as they do, Haynes is heard to mutter that this didn't happen the last time the airline made him go through a flight simulator. Over the resulting laughter, he adds, 'We'll get this thing on the ground, don't worry about it.'

A few moments later, he finds the time to get the name of the off-duty pilot who has come up to the cockpit to offer whatever help he can. The off-duty pilot says he'll buy Haynes a drink when this is over. Haynes replies that he doesn't drink, but after this outing, he'll make an exception.

Choices narrowing all the time and fuel running out, he consults the others on each action before he gives orders, briefing the air hostess on what she's to do if, as he anticipates, the cockpit crew are dead after the crash-landing, laughingly says he'll sign the co-pilot's promotion to full captain if they survive what's coming, cracks a joke to ground control over their generosity in letting him land on any runway at the airport he fancies, takes time to thank everybody for the help they have given – and flies the plane to the ground.

More than two thirds of the 'souls' on board during the catastrophe survived, thanks largely to a captain – who also survived – who knew how to communicate under pressure while creating and maintaining an atmosphere that minimised the chances of anybody panicking.

3   Be careful of small talk

Perhaps the biggest myth of negotiation is that it starts with small talk. In fact, small talk is a pointless and sometimes dangerous exercise. Dangerous because it's during small talk that you are most likely to make a gaffe.

I was involved in that kind of situation many years ago. On a social occasion, clutching my pint glass of 7Up, I was going through the 'what do you do, who do you know, where are you coming from?' social negotiation with a very pleasant man who had already established one useful point of commonality between us: he played golf. We were recalling the better moments of a recent Masters when he suddenly interrupted himself and nudged me, nodding across the crowded room.

'D'you see your one?' he asked, sotto voce.

The nod led to two women talking to each other, one brunette, one very blonde.

'Which one?'

'The dyed blonde.'

I agreed I could see the dyed blonde. He came

slightly closer and his voice dropped even further. The blonde, he told me, glancing from side to side to make sure nobody but I could hear him, was the mistress of a well-known politician. A very well-known politician. I evinced astonishment and interest.

'Did you know she's also my wife?' I asked.

I was sorry the moment I had done it, because the unfortunate man went grey in the face and I thought he might have a heart attack. I laughed, reassured him, and explained he wasn't the first to make the mistake of mushing similar names into a single identity. My wife and I were used to it, I told him. But getting it so wrong put him completely off his stroke, and he left the party early, no doubt fearful that I might introduce him to my wife with glad cries of 'This man thinks you're the mistress of . . . '

In the course of a casual social negotiation, it was a minor and amusing gaffe. It would be neither minor nor amusing if an equivalent inaccuracy were revealed by one side in a serious communication with the other side. Unfortunately, such gaffes do happen at the beginning of a negotiation more frequently than might be expected:

A colleague of mine remembers – with a shudder – a negotiation where, as a small-talk opener, she complimented the owner of a plant on its location, which was exceptionally attractive.

'You're so lucky to work in a lovely place like this,' she added. 'I work on XYZ Road, and it is just so squalid and dirty and dispiriting.'

'I live on XYZ Road,' he replied.

4   Create a professional impact

- Walk as you'd walk to meet your best friend if he/ she had unexpectedly turned up.
- Don't apologise your way across the room. Be purposeful and sure to move to meet or greet other people.
- Keep your head up.
- Don't saunter with hands in pockets.
- Don't weigh yourself down with impedimenta – particularly impedimenta awkward to carry.
- Don't do body-protective gestures like crossing your left hand over to clutch your right arm.
- Learn to walk confidently with your hands by your sides. (Hint: actors are taught to imagine they're carrying heavy glass balls – one in each hand.)
- Keep your head up if you meet someone's eyes. Do a visual: 'I see you and acknowledge you.'
- Keep handshakes firm and short. Avoid the politicians elbow-clutch, the too-familiar double-hand caress or above all, the dead-fish offering.

5   Don't engage in deaf listening and blind looking

When you do 'deaf listening', you are likely to:

- Allow one foot to tap or jiggle.
- Fiddle with small change in your pocket or with the clicker on the end of a pen.
- Permit electronic interruption by cellular phone or tweeting wristwatch.
- Go 'm-m-m', meaning, 'Don't take so long to get to the point, you boring person you.'

'Blind looking' is almost as bad. Although many people look, they do not observe.

They do not observe because we think 'communication' comes to us in packages called 'words'. In point of fact, much communication uses no words at all, just gestures, expressions and physical reactions.

One psychologist has come up with a term for these giveaway communications. He calls them 'tells', because they tell observant viewers something they might otherwise have missed. When selecting juries for major criminal trials in America, both sides frequently employ professionals to spot the 'tells' which indicate suitability or unsuitability for inclusion on the jury panel.

Thus, should the prosecution ask a potential juror if they approve of the death penalty, and the juror affirm that, yes, they do, the expert may point out to the prosecutors that the person being questioned clutched their ear during this answer, unconsciously indicating discomfort.

I have reservations about just how far we should push the interpretation of these little gestures called 'tells', just as I have reservations about the emphasis in much of what is called 'body language training' on noting tiny details liable to be interpreted negatively. The quintessence of this limited and limiting approach is the now-popular cliché that folded arms indicates resistance on the part of the arm-owner to whatever is going on in front of him or her. Gerry Spence, the man who successfully defended Imelda Marcus in

court, having been told about this folded-arm interpretation, says that he worried continually throughout
one trial because a single juror demonstrated it every
day, gradually convincing Spence that his client was for
the high jump.

When the jury returned a verdict favourable to his
client, Spence was so curious that he ran after the big
farmer who had so obdurately folded his arms throughout, and asked him if the posture had been indicative of
resistance to Spence's arguments or personality. The
farmer said it was indicative of neither.

'I gotta big belly,' he pointed out. 'And a man's gotta
put his arms someplace.'

6   Watch out for what's distinctive

When I suggest that we pay attention to what people
say without words, I am not saying that we should be
making notes of tiny features of their body language
interpretable in a negative way. Rather the opposite –
we should look at people to find out what's special
about them or what might give some point of mutual
common interest.

Waiting for the countdown before doing an out-
doors interview for an RTÉ programme, I glanced down
and, during the countdown, registered that the woman
I was interviewing stood in an unusual way. During the
interview, the connection clicked in my mind and
afterwards I asked her how long she had done ballet.
It was just as well I waited until the interview was over,
because she was quite flummoxed that something she
regarded as very much off-line, having nothing to do

with her business or her public self-presentation, should have been detectable.

On another occasion, when facilitating within a company, I noticed that one of the participants, when not actually speaking, had a small repetitive movement of the hands. At first glance, it was nothing more than the normal light drumming of the fingertips on a hard surface, in this case a desk, but in fact, there was a very distinctive recurring sequence to it. Scales, I thought. She's playing scales on a piano. Later, I found that the executive was a fine musician who not only played piano, but harpsichord. To this day, when I meet her, we talk more of music than of business.

Staff in Carr Communications try to improve themselves at this kind of observation. During the first coffee break on one of our monthly Talking Business courses, a customer was startled when the tutor handed him a towel containing a plastic bag filled with frozen peas. A back-sufferer herself, she had spotted his movements as indicative of some back discomfort and was offering the traditional method of numbing inflamed tissues.

Good communicators are either born with – or consciously develop – the skill to note visual messages being sent to them, whether these messages narrate a facet of a life story, make evident a prejudice or preconception or disclose a reaction to what is being proposed. That disclosure must never be overlooked. Someone listening to you may, without words, send subtle physical messages which include:

- Don't belabour that point, I got it ages ago.
- Explain that a bit more. I understand it, I think, but I'm not sure.
- I don't accept that premise for one minute.
- I'm getting worried that you're going to run over time so we won't be able to put questions to you.

7   Listen

Don't talk too much or offer unwanted information about your own organisation. Instead, listen a lot. Some researchers have attempted to establish the proportion of time people at work allocate to reading, writing, talking and listening. They estimate that the largest proportion (just over 40 per cent) is spent listening. They also reckon that only one quarter of listening time is effective. Why?

Because people don't know how to listen productively. Sometimes we listen (or are momentarily quiet) only in order to refute or win a point (this caused me a lot of soul searching when I first reflected on it). The real level that we must reach is listening in order to learn or understand. This listening must include silence but it also leads to the following:

8   Question and probe

Questioning is simple. Any kid can do it. But as we move into adulthood, we suppress our capacity to ask simple questions, motivated by the desire to impress. You hear it all the time on radio programmes, where the interviewer wants to find out what the interviewee did next. The right question is: 'So what did you do next?'

The wrong question is:

So it must have been very hard, in view of what had happened to you, and particularly because of its effects on your children, not that we should ignore how your granny reacted, because you told me before we came on the air how she felt about the issue, but at the same time, there must have been – I assume, anyway – something in you even at that point that would have been saying it was time to move on, time to change, time to take your career and possibly also your domestic life in a radically new direction. Was that the case?'

On a bad day, the interviewee, in response to that kind of 'question' will answer 'Yes' and shut up.

Good questions are short and simple.

Great questions are short, simple, arise out of what has just been said, and sometimes don't need words at all.

If, for example, the financial controller is telling you how the company managed to move from near bankruptcy to substantial profits within one eighteen-month period, the best question may be an indrawn breath (to register the achievement) and the facial expression that says, 'Go on. Tell me more.'

When you're asking questions to find out what makes a company different from the others, you're trying to get light and shade, setback and progress, into the curiously featureless sequence represented by ten-years'-worth of annual reports. Someone once said that trying to get a sense of history by reading news-papers was like trying to work out what time it was by looking at the second hand of a clock. Annual reports have the same drawback, whereas if you have members of the management team in front of you, you can ask the 'differentiator' questions:

- What was the big breakthrough for X Ltd.? (Always use the name of the company and get it right.)
- What was the biggest setback or challenge?
- What are the special strengths of X?
- How are decisions made within X?
- How uniform is the thinking throughout X?
- When there are problems, at what level are they handled?
- How important is the location?
- How are staff rewarded?
- How is morale measured?
- How closely does X's public image match the reality?

Any one of these will get people talking. That does not mean you should ever bring a list of questions to an exploratory session. Start off by asking big open questions, listen to the answers you get and put in follow-up questions.

As a general rule, avoid 'Did you think?' type questions. Instead use 'How?' 'Why?' 'What would happen if ... ' as your stock-in-trade. And keep your follow-up questions open and simple.

- Expand on that for me
- How do you mean, 'unconscionable'?
- For example?
- How did that work out?
- How bad was the result?

Take notes. If you are listening and probing effectively, it is vital that you jot down key words or summaries to have later to reflect on. As soon as you leave the meeting, even in your car in the car-park, fill in some of the detail and the other impressions made on you during the exchanges. Don't be afraid to phone back one of the participants to verify something that you have learned – they may even be flattered by the approach.

Never ignore the obvious.

Good research for a negotiation never churns up the stuff we would expect to see about any company or individual. It is what I call 'Fingerprint Research': it gives us the aspects of a company or individual which distinguish them from anybody else.

ELEMENTARY

Sir Arthur Conan Doyle, the creator of the world-famous detective, Sherlock Holmes, was not above telling tales about himself in which he was the laughing-stock. Here is one of those stories.

As he tells it, he was waiting at a taxi-stand outside the railway station in Paris. When a taxi pulled up, he put his suitcase in it and got in himself. As he was about to tell the taxi-driver where he wanted to go, the driver asked him:

'Where can I take you, Mr Doyle?'

Doyle was flabbergasted. He asked the driver if he knew him by sight.

The driver said, 'No, Sir, I have never seen you before.'

The puzzled Doyle asked him what made him think that he was Conan Doyle. The driver replied: 'This morning's paper had a story about you being on vacation in Marseilles. This is the taxi-stand where people who return from Marseilles always come. Your skin colour tells me you have been on vacation. The ink-spot on your right index finger suggests to me that you are a writer. Your clothing is very English, and not French. Adding up all those pieces of information, I deduce that you are Sir Arthur Conan Doyle.'

Doyle said: 'This is truly amazing. You are a real-life counterpart to my fictional creation, Sherlock Holmes.'

'There is one other thing,' the driver said.

'What is that?'

'Your name is on the front of your suitcase.'

There is nothing so demeaning as to be lumped in with every other vaguely similar company or person, and there's nothing quite so flattering as being identified as different – witness Conan Doyle's delight when the taxi-driver differentiated him from everyone else.

86

TAKEAWAYS

1 Work out what makes a company special and different.
2 Read about the company and talk to people who know it.
3 Meet company representatives on their ground and absorb signals from their environment.
4 Take responsibility for creating atmosphere; get and remember names.
5 Make an impact; listen well.
6 Observe distinctiveness in people.

5

PREPARE WELL

I've outlined how regular a feature negotiation is in our everyday working and family lives and the contexts and misconceptions that sour negotiations. I have categorised a number of approaches which are guaranteed to frustrate the real objective of negotiation and emphasised the behaviours that will lead to successful outcomes, particularly stressing what I've called the four negotiation imperatives. In addition, I have highlighted the depth of research and insight you should have into the distinctive features and values of the organisations and people with whom you communicate.

Now it is time to focus on the actual process of negotiation itself, its antecedents and consequences.

I have divided what you need to do into *four steps*:

- Prepare well
- Plan your approach
- Persuade your colleague
- Protect the outcomes

In his marvellous book, *How to Run Successful Projects – the Silver Bullet*, Fergus O'Connell talks about the *Probability of Success Indication* or PSI. It is an instantaneous measure of how likely or not a project is to succeed. He suggests that not all the ten steps to successful project management are equally important. It is much the same with negotiation. Not all the steps have the same significance. This is the percentage weighting I would give to each negotiation step.

- Prepare well   40
- Predispose for success   10
- Persuade your colleague   30
- Protect the outcomes   20
- Total   100

In other words the crucial steps are to prepare well and persuade your colleague, followed by the need to protect the agreement. Predisposing is not as vital for success.

PREPARE WELL

Most people who negotiate, especially those who think they're good at it, are under the impression that skill during the discussion creates successful outcomes. They are comfortable in their ability to 'wing it,' to respond to what happens, while driving their own agendas. In all the years I have watched people negotiate, heard about interactions or studied videotapes of trainees re-creating real life scenarios, I have never seen that thesis borne out. Of course I have seen people 'not lose'. I have watched negotiators bully or frustrate the other party.

On the other hand, worry is not good preparation, although in Ireland we often confuse the two. Because our stomach may be knotted and we fail to sleep well for several days, we credit ourselves as having done the preparatory work. In fact, unfocused worry is counter-productive. It is the absolute opposite of good preparation.

Its uselessness is best illustrated by the apocryphal story of the man who wants to borrow a ladder from his neighbour. On the way across the road to the neighbour's house, he begins to imagine what the encounter will be like if the neighbour isn't in a good mood. In fact, he figures, the neighbour may not be that willing to be approached for a loan, since a loan of a lawnmower some months back had ended up, after three weeks, with a somewhat chilly request for its return. The would-be borrower, remembering this, begins to suspect that the neighbour, asked another favour, may suggest sarcastically that perhaps buying your own is a good approach to having the tools you need. So the would-be borrower knocks at the neighbour's door in a growing mood of negative anticipation, and when the neighbour opens the door, blurts out 'Why don't you stuff your ladder?' into his astonished face.

Negotiations even for something as simple as borrowing a ladder can be destroyed by engaging in pointless worry instead of doing proper preparation. You don't just arrive in and say to a stranger, 'You and

I have to sort out something.'

My own conviction is that the outcomes of successful, mutually satisfying negotiations are directly related to the quantity and quality of the preparation for them.

FOCUS OF PREPARATION

I cannot stress often enough that effective beneficial negotiations are founded on a fundamental attitude, an attitude that transforms the behaviours throughout the whole transaction. Put very simply, negotiation is the process by which we communicate to get what we want from people who want something from us. It is not about winning or losing. It is not about bowing to pressure or power. Instead it is a collaborative approach to solving shared problems where the goal is a wise outcome reached efficiently and amicably.

FUNDAMENTAL ATTITUDE

The first task in preparation is to examine your own attitude to the process. You will, it is hoped, be confirming that you follow the collaborative model. However a quick reflection on your performance in personal, social or work transactions may alert you to patterns of drift to macho, wimp or personality-based preoccupations. Every time I examine my own tendencies I discover deep-rooted traces of being a control-freak and I have to shake myself loose again.

NEEDS, CONCERNS, INTERESTS

Next you have to think through the needs, concerns or interests that underlie your position and that of the other side on the issue(s) to be discussed. When negotiations break down, reach a stalemate or yield outcomes that are mutually frustrating – 'ashes in the mouth' – it is often a consequence of the incapacity or unwillingness of the participants to understand their true interests. Earlier in the book, I gave examples of the fears or concerns that were the backdrop to specific negotiations. If it is a struggle for you to identify your own real interests it may be worthwhile to look again at those illustrations. It isn't just that people don't express their real needs. As I said earlier, they may have difficulty formulating them in any conscious way. Yet it repays the pain and the effort to do so.

In your preparation not only must you get in touch with your own interests but, crucially, you should have clear ideas about the fears, concerns and interests of the other party. Here is the advice of Dag Hammarskjöld, for me, the most memorable secretary-general of the United Nations: 'You can only hope to find a lasting solution to a conflict if you have learned to see the other party objectively, but at the same time, to experience their difficulties subjectively.'

In other words, it helps to develop your insight and imagination if you have been in the other person's shoes at some time and have learned from the experience. The best way to ensure that you have stretched your creativity on the subject of interests is to write your observations down on paper as part of your preparation. This also provides a checking mechanism for you after the negotiation is completed.

CREATE OPTIONS

The better you become at describing your own interests and those of the other side, the easier it will be to outline a number of options that might satisfy you both.

If an organisation seeks a negotiation with its funding authority to obtain agreement for executives to attend international conferences, while keeping within budget allocations, the available options might be along the following lines:

- Make individual applications to the funding authority for each conference.
- Set out the conferences to be attended for the year and obtain permission en bloc.
- Agree with the funding authority an overall portion of the budget for international conferences and then allow the executives to make their own decisions

When you have worked out a number of options that will meet your needs you should prioritise them. Which best suits your interests, while significantly meeting the needs of the other party? The higher a priority you give to a certain option, the more there is need to prepare the evidence and the supporting detail. Remember you are not trying to win a battle of wills in defence of your preference but appealing to objective criteria and external data that would convince a reasonable other party.

Of the three options given above it would appear that the third one (constituent organisation having proportion of budget for international conferences and power to decide) would be preferable because:

- It saves time and paperwork on both sides – especially compared to option one.
- It allows advanced planning – compared to option one.
- It confirms the freedom and authority of the constituent body – compared to options one and two.
- It gives greater flexibility to executives – compared to option two.

Only through detailed preparation can you deliver value on options suggested. You will notice that the value-added detail should be 'as perceived by the other side'.

Produce Data – Objective Criteria

John is twenty-five and has been working in a medium-sized company for almost three years. He was originally recruited into an administrative clerical role and has more than met the targets and specifications. He feels that he is now engaged in activities with similar responsibilities to those carried out by others with the title Account Executive. He wants to negotiate with the managing director (who decides such things) about being given the new title.

John could adopt a number of approaches to achieving his objective, most of which would not work. In fact they might even be counter-productive in that they could convey to senior management that the company now has a disgruntled employee. However, if he prepares well, particularly by equipping himself with appropriate data and relying on objective criteria, he will maximise his chances of achieving his objective and improving his standing within the company.

John, as part of his preparation, should compile the following:

- The specifications of the job as given to him on recruitment. If he was not given one, he should ask for one or write down the responsibilities he undertook initially.
- A description of the activities he is currently engaged in and the responsibilities he carries.
- A description of the responsibilities and activities of another account executive.
- Records of targets achieved.
- Outcomes from performance appraisals.
- Information on discretionary projects engaged in.

He should also list the benefits to the company from changing his title, such as:

- Greater authority with customers and suppliers.
- Improved motivations for other staff from evidence of career development possibilities.
- Clearer role specification, leading to improved productivity.

Having all this information at his fingertips doesn't mean that John will get the change of role and title he is looking for. Not having them would guarantee that he would be fobbed off with some promise to 'think about' it. Presenting his case in a clear, well-argued, well-documented fashion would help him achieve his objective at least in the medium term and would immediately enhance his reputation with senior management.

For some negotiations, knowing the relevant objective data or criteria takes little effort. For others it requires patience, time and much thought. That is why preparation gets such a high score on the Probability of Success Indicator scale.

ADDRESS ISSUES, NOT EMOTIONS

At first sight, it would seem that you cannot prepare in advance for addressing issues rather than emotions, since that capacity is demonstrated during the actual process. However you should examine your day-to-day track record on this imperative.

The founder and chairman of our company, Bunny Carr, was once asked how susceptible a colleague was to be sidetracked, needled or affected by touches of emotional blackmail. 'A waste of time,' said Bunny, 'you might as well be throwing marshmallows at a cliff.' The individual he talked about is a good negotiator because of his incapacity to be sidetracked or reached by someone trying to play on his emotions. If you do not have that emotional impregnability, remind yourself, before a negotiation, about your penchant for rising to the bait when someone is hostile, stubborn, indecisive – or manifests whichever kind of behaviour might cause you to lose sight of the issue. If you have already dealt with the other party, you should chart likely irritants and commit yourself to specifically different behaviours on your own part.

TAKEAWAYS

1 Preparation is the single most important aspect of negotiation.
2 Prepare according to the four imperatives.
3 Don't make it up as the negotiation unfolds.
4 Examine your fundamental attitude to the negotiation process.
5 Prepare thoroughly on interests, options and objective criteria.
6 Remind yourself about the bait you traditionally rise to.

6

Predispose for Success

I keep six honest serving men
(They taught me all I know)
Their names are What Why and When,
And How and Where and Who.

I send them over land and sea
I send them East and West
But after they have worked for me
I give them all a rest . . .

Rudyard Kipling

Kipling's six serving men have traditionally been the stormtroopers of good journalism. Years ago, as a lecturer in Dublin's Rathmines College School of Journalism, I would listen to students anxiously checking their news stories to see if they had managed to answer all six questions in their opening paragraph, as was required.

The marvellous thing about Kipling's six serving men, however, is that they're great at adapting to different work situations, and they have an enormous role to play in negotiation. They come into their own during the preparatory stage, before the negotiator sits down and sets out to persuade a company or individual to reach a particular point of agreement

I have already dealt with the what, the how, the why and the who of negotiations. The what is the issues. The how is collaboratively problem-solving with a colleague. The why is to achieve mutually acceptable outcomes. The who varies from new companies to other parties you already know. Now I want to use the rest of Kipling's serving men to focus on a few practical issues which should form part of advance planning and predispose for successful outcomes.

WHERE TO NEGOTIATE

Q In the property business, what really matters?
A There are three answers to that. Location. Location. Location.

When it comes to negotiation, while it may not merit a triple repetition, location is nonetheless very important. No matter what the negotiation is. Picture these situations:

- The garda car is parked, blue lights flashing, ahead of the car that's been stopped. The garda is standing beside the other car, pad in hand. He walks around to the front of the car to look at the number plate, then comes back. The driver, throughout, is seated, window open.

- The patient is lying on a trolley in a paper gown which is knotted at the back. The surgeon, talking to the patient, is holding her arms out for a gown to be slipped over her gloved hands.
- The man in the wheelchair is demonstrating to a group of five the features of a building. Sometimes he goes ahead of them; sometimes, having stopped, he twiddles with the electric control of the wheelchair so it moves back and forth about four inches while he talks.
- The woman in the good suit, on her own in a queue in McDonald's, is constantly looking upwards, even when the young man behind the cash register smiles and asks what her order is.

Where is the power in each situation? Where is the comfort?

In the case of the roadside conversation, despite the fact that the car driver is sitting in apparent comfort at the wheel of his own car, both comfort and power clearly rest with the garda. Onlookers make the fair assumption that the garda would not be talking to the driver at the side of the road if the squad car had not flagged down the other car. The implication is that the driver has done something wrong, and since the garda by role is the one to catch wrongdoers, the garda is in an instrumental role, which is reflected by his props (the notebook and the flashing blue lights on the car) and – even more significantly – by his pace. Watch any garda who moves to the front of a stopped car to check its number plate. The pace, invariably, is slow, sending a subliminal message that the garda is in charge of everything, including how much time the driver will spend immobilised.

At first glance, the clothing is not that much different for the surgeon and her patient, but in fact the back-tied surgeon's gown goes over normal clothing, whereas the patient is naked underneath. Nakedness, relative or complete, is hugely contributory to a feeling of loss of authority. In addition, for the time the surgical procedure takes, all of the normally validating information and expertise the patient has is essentially valueless: only medical and specifically surgical skills matter, so the patient is a stranger in a foreign land where they speak a different language.

Again, at first glance, someone in a wheelchair seems at a disadvantage in power terms, because they are of necessity seated and so are at a lower level than the people with whom they deal. In this case, however, the clues indicate otherwise. The wheelchair user is the guide, dictates when the others will move or be still, listen or talk. It is evident, too, that this man is very used to the wheelchair; he has developed an electric habit comparable to a non-wheelchair-user rocking backward and forward on their feet as they talk.

Finally, the woman in the good suit, even though she's more expensively dressed than the young man behind the counter, whose individuality is somewhat reduced by his uniform, is neither comfortable nor in charge. It can be inferred, from her constantly looking up at the menu items listed overhead, that she is unfamiliar with the terms and costs.

What the driver, the patient, the visiting group and the woman in the suit have in common is that they are on someone else's turf. No, I am not suggesting that the garda actually owns the ground on which the driver's car has parked. But by virtue of circumstances, the driver has demonstrably and appreciably less power and control in the situation. He's not playing on his home pitch.

Playing at Home

In sporting terms, playing away is regarded as less advantageous than playing on your home grounds.

If you read the prediction of British soccer results in any newspaper's sporting section, you'd find the number of away wins predicted by the experts in a given week is infinitesimal. For a very good reason. You play better at home in front of your home supporters. So invite the negotiation to your premises, if possible.

Of course, you don't always have the choice. When a public body anywhere in Europe puts a call to tender in the *Official Journal of the European Communities (S Series)* those selected to present to the public body know that there is no possibility of presenting anywhere other than in Brussels or wherever the headquarters of the public body is situated.

However, not all negotiations have so rigid a venue-setting built into them.

When a manager is giving feedback, for example, the session should not necessarily take place in the MD's office, because that means that every time executives subsequently come into the MD's office – when, for example, the MD want them to come in to brainstorm and therefore wants them to feel open and creative – the context may decide otherwise. If the MD's office is inextricably linked in the minds of executives with gruelling performance reviews, it is not the place for a happy brainstorming chat. The associations a venue has may influence quite unrelated proceedings in that venue.

When I mentioned this factor during a course I was giving to a rural health board, one of the psychiatrists said 'You're so right. I remember when the resident medical superintendent was retiring, we were invited into his room for drinks, and I was totally uncomfortable because the only time you were ever in there was when you were in trouble.'

In that specific instance, the resident medical superintendent would have been well advised to invite staff for a drink in a local hostelry, rather than the office which had negative associations for them. That final, unofficial negotiation of parting might have gone marginally better and left warmer memories.

When you have the capacity to decide on the venue, give it some thought. Envisage all the various possibilities and their seen and unseen implications.

PLAYING AWAY

Even when selecting the venue is in your hands, and despite the advantages of playing on your own pitch, never forget the lesson in the phrase 'Your place or mine?' In man–woman relationships, this is not just a casual query.

For example, if she goes to his place, she can always leave, but if she lets him come to her, she has to throw him out. The relationship totally changes depending on whether you go to his place and later say 'I need to go home now' or bring him to your place and have to say 'I don't want you here in the morning.' That's difficult. It may warp the whole relationship. 'Your place or mine?' has more implications than the simple one of whether or not there is an available place.

Even if you have to play on someone else's pitch, you can still go a long way towards turning that pitch into home ground. I always advise people who are making a formal presentation as part of the negotiations to check out the setting in advance.

- How big is the room?
- What's the technology?
- Where do people sit?
- When the blinds are pulled, what's the visibility?
- Where are the sockets?

If several people are to present, what's the best choreography for their movements: where should they start and where should they go after they've spoken so they don't crash into each other?

A good host company will always telephone and ask what technology would be preferred by the people making the presentation. Although this is meant to be helpful, it is sometimes interpreted by the recipients of the call as instructive, rather than information-seeking – 'Oh, they expect us to use PowerPoint!' – and may pressure the presenters into using technology with which they are unfamiliar. You should resist the pressure. Instead, the objective should be to make an 'away' pitch as familiar and comfortable as possible.

Even if you are on someone else's turf, you can make yourself very comfortable – in subtle ways, rather than the way Bill Murray does it in the film *Quick Change*. At the beginning of that movie, Murray, a bank robber dressed up as a clown, arrives at a bank at closing time, when a security man is trying to get all remaining customers out. Encountering this red-nosed clown, the security man says 'You, too, Bozo.' Producing a handgun, the clown gestures him out of the way, and adds, to the now terrified security man, '*Mister* Bozo to you.' It's a very funny example of taking ownership of the territory.

More subtle indicators are where someone deploys their files and/or props comfortably and in an un-hurried way. In this, the negotiator is always helped by minimalism. A briefcase is better than a sliding armful of separate items likely to cascade to the floor in wild disarray.

When it is a one-to-one negotiation, much is often made of the presence or absence of a table between the two negotiators.

The first time I encountered the table-as-ploy was when a friend was negotiating a new contract with her employer, and, experiencing great difficulty with her immediate boss, sought an interview with the chief executive of the large organisation involved. She was shown into his office, where he was seated behind his desk, completing a phone call. With a welcoming wave, he invited her to sit in the chair facing him across the desk. She did so. But when he finished the phone call, he pulled his own chair around the desk, so they were both on the same side.

The young woman involved was warmed by the removal of the physical obstacle, and confided her problems in the boss. He listened attentively, promised to do whatever he could, and they parted amicably. Later, she mentioned what she had done, in confidence, to an older executive in the same organisation.

'Don't tell me,' the older executive said. 'He came right around the desk and sat on the same side of it as you were sitting and you thought what a warm accessible human being. Right?'

With a sinking feeling in the pit of her stomach, she nodded.

'Does it all the time,' he smiled. 'Works perfectly – the first time. But then, he makes sure there's never a second time.'

'How does he do that?' she asked, the sinking feeling worsening.

'Promises to do anything he can,' her friend said. 'Of course, he can't do anything because he so strongly believes in delegation of authority, but people wait in hope. After all didn't God come right around the desk to talk to us lesser mortals?'

I would regard that as a poor negotiation from the CEO's point of view, because not only was the trick exposed by overuse but the sense of having been manipulated ensured that the individual on the other side of the negotiation was a quietly sworn enemy from that point onward. Which in turn meant that a door had been closed on any future negotiation with that person.

I don't, personally, place great importance on this strategy of 'taking away the obstacle' of a table. I think there should be a table between people. Partly as a working surface, partly as a way to separate people and give them space not to be intimidated. A table, especially if it is a fairly sizeable table, allows both sides of a negotiation to lay out their papers in the confidence that the other side cannot read their notes. It also gives that extra space conducive to reflection and thought.

When to Negotiate

Once the *where* has been established, the next issue is the *when*.

Now this one often constitutes an insoluble problem, because although most of us have times of the day at which we are more reasonable and amenable, we are unlikely to broadcast that schedule in any location where the information might be useful to a future negotiator. Even if a negotiator knows the time of the day at which the individual on the other side of the negotiation is at their best, they are unlikely to be able to ensure that this is the time the negotiation is scheduled for. In my own company, we have one group of people who are 'larks', who love to come to work before the traffic builds up. Some of them routinely start at six in the morning or earlier. They are balanced by 'owls' like myself, who will happily work until nine or ten at night.

Were an outsider negotiating with us to suggest a working breakfast, that would push all of the buttons of some of our people but might irritate the rest.

In tendering situations, I believe a shared toss of the dice to be the best way to allocate times to different tenderers. This would obviate a lot of pointless jockeying.

In one-to-one negotiations within a company, on the other hand, a tug at the corporate grapevine and a little personal observation can yield rich fruits of information about best and worst times. Some bosses will give you anything if you talk to them on the Friday before a long weekend, others are particularly positive after a lunch with a particular client.

One woman manager told me recently that she never slates crucial negotiations for the two or three days before she expects to menstruate.

'I don't believe in PMS as an illness or a disability,' she said firmly. 'But I have enough insight into my own thinking process to know that just before my period, I go through a time of heightened responses to everything. I don't believe that's necessarily the best frame of mind to be in when I'm negotiating something complex and subtle that will have to stick for a long time and which will have considerable implications for everybody within the company, so I schedule around it. Just as I schedule important negotiations so as not to put any of the management at the table directly after a flight from HQ in

Oregon. The time zones mean they're going to be jet-lagged, and even those who are used to long-distance flights west to east experience an ill-defined shift of focus which would not put them in the best mode to negotiate.

QUESTIONS OF TIMING

The more problematic aspect of the *when* question is the length of time between, for instance, a call to tender and actual negotiation. You get the call to tender on a Friday. You must have your submission on their desk in triplicate by the following Wednesday. When the submission is a hundred-page, tightly typed, heavily researched and unit-costed proposal, then the length of time proposed can appear somewhat constrained.

'At this stage we know,' a partner in one of the big accountancy partnerships commented, 'when a major body invites us to tender for an audit and gives us that kind of notice, that they are putting it out to tender because the law, their constitution or some regulation says they must. But they have no intention of giving the audit to anybody other than the present incumbent. It stands to reason that only the present incumbent would have sufficient information and time at their disposal to do a professional job of the presentation, support documentation and negotiation.'

When given such short notice, the man I quote thanks the sender of the call, indicates that the chance to work for such a (fill in the dotted encomiastic line yourself) company would be mighty, says that the partnership would be delighted to tender if the company were prepared to give more time to the tendering process, because that is the amount of time the partnership believes should be devoted to a fully professional examination of the client's needs, and that if the client company can't give those extra days, the partnership wishes them continued success and the services of a top-notch accountancy firm.

On one occasion, the response to this letter was a startled phone call from the client company, indicating that they were flattered to death by the willingness of the partnership to devote that much time to the pitch, and their request for extra time was granted. They also won the contract. More regularly, however, the response is a courteous blank wall: meet the deadline or be struck off the list.

Sometimes, when the call to tender is going to public relations companies, the rationale behind a tight deadline is not that the client wants to hang on to the PR agency it currently uses, but a more sophisticated one. The client is saying 'If you were my PR consultants, you would have to move like lightning if we had an emergency at the plant or a sudden profits warning. The only real way to gauge your capacity to respond at that kind of speed is to give you an unreasonable deadline. You want the job, you meet the deadline.'

In a competitive situation where there is a deadline, do not send in your documentation a day in advance to prove how on-the-ball you are. That may be a good approach if you are submitting a commissioned feature to a newspaper, but in any properly run organisation, the proposal that arrives early is usually filed in an in-tray, unopened until it is joined by competitor documentation. In a crookedly-run organisation, early documentation gets opened and vital bits of information leaked to one or more of the competitors. Meet the deadline comfortably and no more than that.

Accepting the invitation gives experience of every aspect of the negotiation process from advance planning to post-negotiation written follow-up. This experience can serve as a helpful dry-run for subsequent negotiations where the odds are not quite so negatively stacked. In addition, there may be a hidden long-term benefit. This time around, the key buying influence may be the boss, and he or she may be joined at the hip to a competitor supplier. However, sitting powerlessly on the panel may be someone who in a few years time will be the boss, and that person will remember a gallant and highly professional job done against all the odds and will be positively predisposed towards the company which did that job.

CLEARLY ESTABLISH LEVELS OF AUTHORITY

In predisposing for success, deal with one other problem before the actual negotiation begins – establish precisely the level of authority each person has to come to agreement.

In a strategic sales negotiation, for example, you want to know if the person in front of you is the key buying influence (KBI) or not. In training computer sales representatives in a number of European countries we discovered a pitfall: the sales rep took as a given that the head of information technology was their KBI, whereas in many cases, the head of IT was at least matched, and sometimes exceeded, in buying power and influence by the financial controller.

The reps, having met all the needs of the IT head, were floored when they did not always get the order: the finance figure they might not even have met, let alone identified as a KBI, blocked the purchase because it failed to meet expenditure specifications although it had met technical specifications.

In addition to feeling floored, the sales reps also commonly felt betrayed by the head of IT. In this, they were not justified, since they had failed to investigate the situation. If the head of IT did not choose to downgrade himself in their eyes, but instead signed off on the technical specifications with them – and with their competitors – in the knowledge that the final veto was in the hands of the finance man, that is understandable. The reps themselves were responsible for the inadequate interrogation of the context in advance of the final negotiation.

The first thing you need to do is find out what power the other person has to negotiate and what status they have because you may go through all the process with one person only to have them say to you, 'Well, I would agree with you, but I have to go back and talk to my boss.'

Find out and verify the level of influence and authority of the person you are dealing with. If you're going to make an agreement that will change the basis of their operation, can this person do that or do they have to go to somebody else? If they say, 'No I can't make that decision, you'll have to ask someone else', it is much better that they say it early in the negotiation rather than later. Clarity on this issue means that you may, for example, seek to meet the more authoritative person early on to find out where they are at. It may also mean that you leave more information in writing with the less authoritative person, on the basis that people tend inadvertently to taint or misinterpret information as they pass it on verbally, and so your material has a better chance of accurately reaching the pivotal person if you do not place excessive reliance on the intermediary's capacity to pass it on.

A bank manager recently told me of a negotiation he had undertaken with a figure well known in regional industry. Let's call him Barney Grinder. Grinder came in to discuss the skewed finances of the Dungbuckets company, of which Barney was known to be a director, but was not so in name.

When all the negotiation cards had been dealt, and when the two of them were in perfect amity on the future progress of delinquent payments, Barney said to the bank manager, 'You know of course, I'm not chief executive and I have no officer status in this company at all. I'll have to go back and talk to them and I don't know what their reaction will be.'

'What did you do?' I asked the bank manager.

'What could I do? ' he shrugged.

'Here's what you could have done,' I told him. 'You could have said, 'Barney, don't gimme that. The dogs in the street know that you've no executive position, but that you still call the shots. Now are you telling me that you're for this or not, never mind what your official status is?"

Knowing that Barney Grinder prides himself on direct talking and on calling a spade a spade, the bank manager laughed as he imagined the conversation progressing.

'You knew his status when you started dealing with him,' I reminded the bank manager. 'So you needed to call him on it, rather than giving him an extra card to play. He now has a card to play which is that he can come back and shrug and say 'Well, I was very much for it, but the rest of the lads wouldn't wear it.' You needed to sort that out, not at the end of the negotiation but at the beginning. 'Barney, if we come to an agreement, can you deliver on it? No? Well, if you can't, who can? Joe? Right, then, how soon can we sit down with Joe?' Or if Barney Grinder acknowledges where he's really coming from, and says, "Oh, no, if I agree it with you, it'll stick," then you're on sure ground.'

Clear the authority of the person as early as you can. In non-sales negotiations, this is just as important as in sales negotiations, even occasionally determining which person will outline their proposals first.

Normally if you're in a higher status role than the other person, you're at liberty to decide whether you'll go first in making the pitch, or let them go first to outline whatever it is that they're looking for.

Takeaways

1 Think about the best location for meeting the needs of both sides.
2 There are advantages in the home venue.
3 If you can, familiarise yourself in advance with an away venue.
4 Know the timing that puts you at a disadvantage.
5 Don't negotiate with conflicting agendas.
6 Know the levels of authority on both sides.

7

PERSUADE YOUR COLLEAGUES

You have prepared well. Now we come to the actual process of negotiation.

- You know your real needs, concerns or interests, and you have some insight into the needs, concerns and interests of the other party.
- You have developed a range of options, which will meet those fundamental needs and you have prioritised those options.
- You will bring to the transaction evidence rather than assertions and will know the objective criteria that will preclude a battle of wills.
- Throughout the encounter the focus will be on issues not emotions and people will be separated from the problem.

Connect all those to a conviction that you and the other negotiator are colleagues seeking wise outcomes to shared problems and you have all the ingredients for success. That's why the title of this chapter is

Persuade Your Colleagues. It serves as a reminder that you're in the persuasion business and not that of objections, challenges and debates.

Studying different styles of negotiation, not long ago, I came across a negotiator widely regarded as the best in the business at coping with objections. Analysing what he was doing, it seemed to me – and I put it to him – that he was constantly moving other people out of the objector box into the explainer box. He laughed.

I suppose that *is* what I'm doing, but you're putting an awful lot of finesse around something I did from the very beginning, because I didn't know any better. I knew nothing. I was scared of the other side and the only aim I had was not to be thrown out. I knew if they kept talking, they wouldn't get around to throwing me out, so every time it looked like they were coming to a conclusion, especially a hostile conclusion, I'd say I didn't follow – and that would get them talking again. Half the time I think they talked themselves into good humour.

But in the process, I realised with a great sense of relief that negotiation is not about talking, it's about getting the other guy to talk. I suppose you're right, I do these days try to get people out of the objector box and into the explainer box. But I'll tell you something else I've discovered. People prefer explaining to fighting, and if they explain in enough detail to someone who's paying attention, there will be some clues in their explanation – clues to a possible solution.

Instead of the 'Hell, this is a hand grenade' response, this man has a 'Hey, this is a bag of goodies' response to an incoming objection. It is something to be explored with interest and openness, not rejected with instant contradiction. His mental attitude is reflected in his physique. I have watched him facing what appeared to be insurmountable objections, and if you turned down the sound, you would assume he was listening to the Lottery numbers to check if he was among this week's winners: sitting forward, no tension in the face, expression curious and attentive, relaxed hands on desk.

This is in sharp contrast to many negotiators, who, even when they control their verbal response to an objection, don't control their physical response. Here are just some of the dead give-aways, the physical 'tells' demonstrated by negotiators under pressure in front of our cameras:

- Blushing
- Clenching of hands
- Aversion of gaze
- Mouth closed, breathing heavily through nose
- Clicking end-clicker on pen
- Audibly dry mouth
- Sweating

Physical 'tells' can be counter-productive in a negotiation – as, indeed, can any behaviour or communication which is outside the control of the negotiator. They tend to create a self-defeating circle of feedback.

SUGGESTIONS FOR EFFECTIVE PERSUASION

1   *Negotiate the non-contentious first*

There are ways of ordering priorities at the beginning of a negotiation which can allow a relationship to develop before it is necessary to hit a wall of potential disagreement. This kind of order is valid and straightforward, not phoney.

If you are setting out to create a positive environment for discussion, and you know that some, but not all of the issues are going to be contentious, you start to negotiate small, easy ones first. Begin in the areas where you can achieve things. Instead of going first to the contentious issues, say, 'Before we start, can we clear up the thing about so-and-so, there's a bit of confusion about that and they're getting very worried here. Can you sort that out? You can? Great. I'm delighted. That gets that out of the way. And there's one other small thing I want also to clarify.'

By concentrating initially on the areas of probable agreement, in essence you are training the two sides to work together. You are getting a sense that 'You and I can get together to solve problems' before you come to the hard questions.

2   *On contentious issues, agreeing in principle can start things moving*

Imagine the following scenario where Adrian wants to negotiate with Frances, his immediate boss, about the conditions under which he and his colleagues are working. Kicking off the meeting, Adrian gives:

- a statement on poor overall conditions – too many people working in three illogically allocated rooms
- an outline of the difficulties faced by incoming customers
- a sense of the problems of concentration for individual staff and the impact on phone conversations with suppliers and customers
- some comments on unkept promises made previously for improvement
- reference to the more salubrious conditions of supervisors/managers

Frances moves into quick reply by:

- restating the overall financial status of the organisation and the facts about budget allocations
- spelling out the reality of 'no other spare accommodation' within existing premises
- stressing the need to keep staff together in one location
- highlighting the importance of people in the three rooms keeping close to support services like faxes, photocopying etc.
- Dealing with the 'promises' issue by reference to

> unexpected growth in business and recruitment of
> new staff

This negotiation can quickly founder, with time being spent on point-scoring, self-justification, threat, counter-threat and mutual frustration.

Instead, the two sides should seek agreement in principle on some issues, thus:

- Agree that current conditions are unacceptable.
- Define or start the process of defining criteria for room occupancy.
- Agree that there are long-term and short-term problems.
- Agree in principle a commitment to finding a long-term solution. Work out specifics later on.

Agreement on principles and criteria ensures that efforts to resolve the short-term problems are perceived as genuine rather than as cynical palliatives. That achieved, Adrian and Frances could then focus on constructive, collaborative options to ameliorate short-term difficulties, such as office sharing with managers/supervisors, utilising desks of flexitime staff, examining possibilities of relocating back-office support services.

3 Concentrate

People with fidgety minds make poor negotiators and even poorer poker players. If I were to name a good attribute for a negotiator, I would plump for the ability to concentrate over long periods of time.

The capacity to concentrate allows the negotiator to focus on small details while never losing sight of the big picture. It allows for clarification and regular summaries of what has been achieved, while at the same time allowing the negotiator to make an immediate concession in the interests of a long-term objective.

4   Listen to understand

The course at Carr Communications with the best track record in improving the success rate of client companies in pitching for new business is not a Presentation Skills or a Selling Skills course. It is a Listening Skills programme.

We videotape an initial exploratory meeting – the kind of meeting the senior partner in an accountancy or legal partnership might have with the MD of a prospective client firm in order to ascertain the needs of the potential client.

When it comes to playback, the individual doing the information-seeking is always surprised to find how many things were actually said that they did not hear, did not notice or did not explore or probe. The reasons are many, but the most frequent cause is two-fold. The questioner:

1 Is too eager to sell, so takes any opportunity to push their firm at the expense of gaining information about the client firm.
2 Does not know how to listen.

Not knowing how to listen, explore and probe is lethal in negotiation. It causes negotiators to lose or not recognise much of the material on which real solutions could be based.

5 Ask good questions

As I said earlier, good questions are short, simple and open. Great questions are short, simple, open and arise out of what has been said.

6 Take notes

It takes an extraordinary talent to keep in your head all the data, by-plays, options and problems that creep up during a negotiation. Notes are not just for follow-up purposes. They are the guidelines for the effective summarising on which so much depends.

7 Welcome resistance

When I was growing up, my father, a stonemason, would often press me into service when he was erecting a fence. My job was to hold the fence posts while he hammered them in. If a post went in very easily, he would immediately order me to take it out again.

'Why?' I would ask, having been delighted with the way the post sank home.

'Not enough resistance,' he'd say. 'The minute I put barbed wire on it, it'll pull out of that soft soil. You need resistance.'

In a negotiation, it's not resistance that should deflate you. It's meeting no resistance. Because if everything you say is agreed to at first go, the chances are that it's going into soil that's too soft and will pop out very quickly. You need resistance.

Just as it is an axiom of war that you should never interrupt an enemy committing suicide, it should be an axiom of negotiation that you should never interrupt someone on the other side of the table when they're in the process of working their way around to your way of thinking. Resistance may be the first sign that they're beginning to take seriously what you are proposing.

Paying attention to resistance may require the curbing of instinctive responses. When someone says: 'I'd like to go with that strategy, but it's too complex,' the instinctive response is along these lines: 'It's not actually that complex. If you went with the X strategy, you'd quickly find yourself up to your armpits in complexities.'

Contradiction is an instinct. Contradiction is rarely persuasive. Instantaneous contradiction is never persuasive, because it is heard by the other person as: 'You stupid dork, you're wrong. You're so obviously wrong.'

However ineffective contradiction may be, it is a reflex, not unlike the reflex a soldier displays when an enemy tosses a hand grenade into the sandbagged bunker in which the soldier is hiding: he catches it and throws it back.

That instinct serves the soldier well. In the negotiator it must be redirected. Instead, the negotiator must do something deeply unnatural: ask interested questions about it.

'Complexities – clarify that one for me?'

'Where are the complexities you'd prefer were not involved?'

This response is respectful of the other and does not pretend that you know every facet of their thinking. It also gives you specifics to deal with, and keeps all conduits of communication open. As you progress, you may ask another question about the first part of the statement, 'I'd like to go with that strategy, but it's too complex.'

Your problem-solving colleague has said they would like to go with this strategy. Why? If they expand on that point, they are putting both negatives and positives on the table and the two of you can then work out the best balance between the red lights and the green lights.

8   Communicate benefits

Fatal to any negotiation is the misconception that because you believe something passionately, because a particular truth is obvious, not to say inescapable as far as you are concerned, it must have the same effect on the person with whom you're negotiating.

This is a failure of empathy – an assumption that the other person's way of thinking and priorities are less cogent than one's own, and that, presented with the evidence in any form, the other person will acknowledge the failure in their thinking or behaviour up to this point and undergo a total conversion.

Arguably the most tragic personification of this failure of empathy was an eighteenth-century physician named Semmelweiss. This man observed that the death rate among new mothers was sharply different when the two wings of the Viennese maternity hospital where he worked were compared with each other. In one wing, very few mothers died of 'childbed fever' as puerperal fever was then known. In the second wing, women died like flies.

Intrigued by this, he realised that the wing with the calamitous morbidity and mortality records was the one staffed by highly qualified surgeons, whereas the wing where mothers who had just given birth had a markedly better chance of surviving was run by midwives. This made no sense, since midwives at the time were illiterate and without standing in the medical community. Semmelweiss embarked on the nineteenth-century version of work study, observing how patients in each section were cared for, and noted that the surgeons undertook one procedure from which the midwives were rigidly precluded: the autopsy. Surgeons dissected dead bodies, and went directly from handling cadavers to conducting physical examinations of women who had given birth. Their progress from the first to the second task was not interrupted by any handwashing. Long before Pasteur adduced the principles of sepsis and anti-sepsis, Semmelweiss worked out that the surgeons were picking up and transporting something on their hands from working with corpses and that this was proving lethal to the women patients they subsequently handled.

It was a breathtaking insight and a statistically-supportable point, and so Semmelweiss embarked on a campaign to change the practices of the male surgeons. Success in his negotiation with them would have prevented hundreds of thousands of deaths in the succeeding years, not to mention obviating a level of suffering difficult now to imagine. Yet the deaths and the suffering went on for decades after he hit on the truth because he could not comprehend that his own personal conviction would not be instantly accepted by others.

If he had thought at all about where the surgeons were coming from, there were three substantial obstacles to their acceptance of his theories.

The first was the change obstacle. The surgeons would have had to change attitudes and behaviours – and, even where there is much evidence to support such a change (as is the case with giving up cigarettes, for example) it is nonetheless difficult to alter the habits of a lifetime.

The second obstacle was loss of prestige. The surgeons of the day regarded midwives as the lowest form of paramedical life, and the notion that, in puerperal fever prevention, it was midwives who were delivering best practice would have been very hard to take.

The third obstacle was the implicit invitation to condemn themselves as murderers: not usually a good opening move in any negotiation.

Semmelweiss, fuelled by the horrific truth of his study, essentially launched into a full-frontal assault on the self-esteem of the surgeons, portraying them as killers. Helped by his level of physical disorganisation and poor communication, the medical establishment decided he was half-mad and wholly rejectable. He spent twenty fruitless years fighting the medical establishment and died in an asylum. It was left to the mild-mannered and presentable Joseph Lister to persuade the medics that scrubbing and disinfecting were fundamental to safe surgery.

The Semmelweis case is just one example of someone with something of major value to contribute being stymied by their own passion and lack of empathy. If you want to persuade someone to change the way they do their job or conduct their business, you must start from where they are at, and you must demonstrate the benefit to them of making the desired changes.

9   *Watch your language*

Selecting the right language for negotiation means using the descriptions preferred by your colleague across the table. Men in their fifties tend to refer to females as 'ladies'. Fair enough. Until they are negotiating with feminists, who find the term 'ladies' judgemental and patronising. Members of the travelling community do not call themselves 'itinerants' and a negotiator who uses that term in dealing with them is using an inappropriate term, just as a negotiator who calls someone a 'non-Catholic' rather than a 'Protestant' is creating – through language – a negative context for the negotiation.

The rule is simple: call people by what they call themselves.

Here's another rule: KYOS. Keep Yourself Off Stage.

Or, to put it another way, egocentric language is unhelpful in negotiation.

When sentences are peppered with:

- I
- Me
- Mine

that's egocentric language.

A third rule for language in negotiation: Don't use emotive terms.

If someone in the Middle Ages dressed in chain mail, the message delivered to any observer by their gear was that they were intending to go to war. No observer would look at a chain-mailed man and assume 'Oh, right, he's off to milk his cow.'

We have precisely the same reaction to language. When someone dresses up in bellicose language, we probably make the assumption that they're going to war and we are thus likely to get dressed up in matching verbiage.

If, on the other hand, detached, third-person language is used, there is a much greater chance of reaching agreement:

It could be argued that the best situation would be where –

Not

If you don't do X, I'm damned if we'll do Y.

Language doesn't have to be emotive or aggressive to cause problems. Recently I watched a negotiation between the representative of a funding authority and a representative from one of the bodies being funded. The discussion was very civilised, without any traces of incipient rancour. Then the former happened to say, 'When we are dealing with subservient organisations . . .' The rest of his sentence and meaning were lost on the listener, who reddened in response to the perceived insult: subservient.

10 Deal with the data, not the emotion

This would seem, at first glance, merely a variation on the earlier theme of addressing the issue, not the person. But there's more to this one. In the middle of a negotiation, the person or people on the other side of the table – your colleagues in future consensus – may throw you a curve ball, or a negative input freighted with emotion.

An example, from outside the business world:

When our son, Anton, was a teenager, he had a lively social life. So lively, in fact, that his mother became convinced he was going to fail every exam he had to sit. (He didn't.) When she would encounter him coming in late at night in term time, she would go on the attack.

'Where the hell were you until this hour of the morning?' she would demand.

Inevitably, Anton would respond to the emotional outrage being expressed and would go into a rant about his rights, about how nobody else his age had to undergo this third degree when they came home a bit later than normal and a lot else besides. Battle would be joined and nobody would be speaking for a week.

Then I taught Anton this rule of negotiation.

'Deal with the informational part of the question,' I said. 'Not the emotive part.'

Because he is the fastest learner around, the next time he was asked what had kept him out so late, his answer was neutral in tone and heavy in information.

Well, he began, he had first of all been up with Rea Lydon, looking at Rea's brother's car, which Rea's brother was thinking of selling before he went back to college in the autumn. Then he went around to see Peter Tuite, and Peter's father had promised him a lift home, but because Peter's father was a vet and had got called out to a cow calving in Malahide, by the time he came back it was half twelve, and so . . .

It may not have solved the time-keeping problem, but it certainly solved the mother–son emotional conflict problem.

So: deal with the data part of an issue, not the emotive part.

11   Bypass irrelevancies

Your company was ripped off eight months ago, and the auditors say the fraud was the company's fault. You're from a division which has nothing to do with the area wherein the fraud happened, but today, in the middle of a negotiation with a client, she makes a snide reference to the fraud, implying that your entire organisation is crooked.

This approach is a means of distracting a negotiator into taking their eyes off the ball. Don't rise to the bait. Don't explain, defend or resent what has been said. Because the other division is of no moment in the current negotiation, the only safe response is a raised eyebrow and a smile, indicating, 'You're teasing me. We have more important things to achieve here today, don't you think?'

This technique is called 'turning a blind eye', although not many people remember the first person who turned a literally blind eye on a distraction. In the middle of a naval battle, Lord Nelson was told that the ship holding a naval officer senior to himself was signalling that Nelson's ship was to draw back from the action in which it was engaged. Nelson, who was blind in one eye, turned and solemnly looked at the signalling ship with the eye that didn't work, and when he understandably failed to see the signal, went on doing exactly what he had been doing all along. As a negotiating tactic in a world of smoke, blood and signals, it was superb – and worth translating into modern negotiation contexts.

12 Know when to stop

There are three danger zones in negotiations when red lights should come on in the head.

- The first is when you hit the target early.
- The second is when they are doing less well than expected.

- The third is when the negotiation has terminally run out of steam.

Although we all know that when you're in a hole, you should stop digging, some negotiators do not understand that the corollary is also true; when you're at the top of the ladder, stop climbing.

I once worked out a strategy with an Irish radio producer which was to get a large British regional station interested in a package he believed would inject new vigour into their output. After our first discussions, he went away and did a lot of homework, not just about the station, but about the person within the station who would make the final decision. He even managed to winkle out her direct office phone number. Planning the negotiation, he decided on a two-pronged approach with a high-risk opener. Knowing that she started very early each morning, before her secretary arrived, he would telephone the direct line just before eight o'clock and give her just enough of his package, verbally, to whet her appetite. He would then seek a meeting to make a detailed, costed presentation to her.

Halfway through the day which was to start with him phoning her, he called me. He had rung her, pitched to her, and she had asked some questions. There had been a long silence before she said, 'OK. How soon can you start and what'll it cost us?'

'I bloody nearly said to her, "No, you don't understand, I have to give you this presentation that I've worked out," he told me. He just about managed to restrain himself, but winning the whole negotiation without having to do phase two was unsettling to him. He had a need to go through the whole performance. However, as he quickly reminded himself, a negotiation is a process, not a performance. If it achieves what it is setting out to achieve before Act Two, bring down the curtain.

The second danger – what if, before Act One is even completed, the negotiator has run out of material? It happens. It should not happen, but it happens. When it happens, the right course of action is to seek an adjournment and indicate that when you meet again, you will have more added value to offer, more good stuff to put on the table. Then make sure you have what you promised.

The third danger is where two sets of interests which ideally should be converging, or at least running in parallel, are clearly becoming more, rather than less divergent. Some negotiators become so addicted to the concept of consensus that they lose sight of the objective in their resolute reinforcement of the relationship. If the objective is unreachable, then there comes a time when the relationship should be put on the back burner, to be brought to boiling point some other time, some other place, on some other issue of mutual interest.

When John De Lorean, the car designer, was negotiating with the Industrial Development Authority to set up a manufacturing plant in the Republic of Ireland, he was simultaneously negotiating with their opposite numbers in Northern Ireland. This direct competition, while not unfamiliar to the development bodies concerned, does tend to heighten the sense of playing for high stakes, and when the IDA folded their negotiating tent, indicating that they had made their final offer and would go no further, their competitors must have been delighted. A couple of years later, when the De Lorean plant in the North folded, leaving grant-aid debts of millions, having produced a handful of grossly over-weight and technically flawed, if visually pleasing vehicles, the IDA thanked their lucky stars that they had been clearheaded enough to call a halt when they did. Someone once said of a notorious bore that, in conversational terms, 'he got on without knowing where he was to get off.' In negotiation, don't ever get on without knowing where you're going to get off.

TAKEAWAYS

1 Don't confuse yourself trying to remember and act out too many logistics.
2 Achieve some 'wins' for both sides at the beginning of a negotiation.
3 On contentious issues, look for agreement in principle as a starting point.
4 Concentrate.
5 Listen to the words and between or underneath the words.
6 Ask probing questions.
7 Take notes – they help the summaries which act as resting points before further progress.
8 Welcome resistance.
9 Concentrate on benefits.
10 Use appropriate language.

11 Learn to empathise: to walk in the other person's shoes.

12 Know when to stop – don't fear deadlock.

8

PROTECT THE OUTCOMES

In an earlier chapter, we looked at the political case study of the agreement reached between former Taoiseach Albert Reynolds and former Tánaiste Dick Spring in relation to the appointmentas President of the High Court of Harry Whelehan in 1994. Other matters were agreed on at the same meeting but the public was never to see them come to fruition because the government collapsed in December of that year. Ultimately, the agreement did not work because adequate arrangements were not made to protect it.

When you reach agreement make sure:

- you are absolutely precise about what has actually been agreed
- you specify who has to deliver what elements in what way
- both parties are clear about any conditions that apply
- you clarify any assumptions that underpin the agreement

- you have agreed deadlines by which compliance must occur
- you indicate precisely what, if any, contingencies have been allowed for

The moment a negotiation is complete, ideally before you part from your colleague, you should document exactly what precisely has been agreed. In some cases this will involve a very formal written agreement. But even in negotiations, which might never have the significance of the Tinakilly discussions, the written confirmation is vital. If, for example, you have participated in one of those 'unacknowledged' negotiations in your own workplace you should send a memo to your colleague outlining the outcomes precisely.

An oral understanding is not worth the air it's written on. Written follow-up is crucially important to the success of negotiations, because it puts on record what has been agreed and what has not.

Confirmation of an agreement in written form is always welcome to the other party if the negotiation has been undertaken in good faith, because this follow-up document can move the process along. It can contain precise instructions as to who does what next and what the agenda is for the next encounter. Piece by piece, you're moving everything forward to implementation.

Protecting a successful negotiation requires a multiplicity of actions, depending on the context and issues involved.

COMMUNICATING TO THE UNINVOLVED

Explaining the results of a negotiation to one's own side can be just as difficult as reaching a consensus in the first place. At the end of one negotiation where I served as facilitator, one side asked for a continuation on a different issue, with only the two top men present. This was agreed, and work resumed. The issue? Mr B had – because it was the right thing to do in everybody's interests – made a number of concessions. If Mr A went public and indicated that the concessions had really come from only one side, said Mr B, the agreement would fail. Mr A began to get very red in the face. I could see he had been looking forward to a little boasting on the business pages, and perhaps an editorial in a newspaper of record praising the resolute stance he had taken.

Mr B laid it out factually and bleakly. His post within his organisation was coming up for re-election. If he was seen to have made concessions, he had no chance of winning. But if he lost, the contender who would take over would repudiate the agreement without hesitation – indeed, would have to repudiate the agreement to prove himself a stronger negotiator than Mr B. Therefore, the instant gratification of a headline might cost Mr A the ultimate gratification of the agreement holding firm.

As Mr B talked, Mr A began arguably the most complex negotiation any of us do: the negotiation with self. It was easy to guess some of the questions he was asking himself; because he was once again trying to work out where his real interests lay in regard to this unexpected development:

- Is this guy (Mr B) just using this as a ploy to prevent my side getting the credit it deserves?
- If I don't take credit, will it weaken my own position?
- Do I want Mr B to continue in office, or do I care?
- Do I believe his successor would repudiate what has been agreed?
- Is there any way I can quietly put out the word that this was a success?

To protect a successful negotiation, he eventually agreed to Mr B's proposals.

In essence what had taken place was a new process of negotiation on how the outcomes were to be communicated – during which the same core principles and approaches applied as for the original negotiation.

COMMUNICATING OUTCOMES WITH MEDIA

In the aftermath of a negotiation, an immediate task is to inform one's own side and make sure that they understand the advantages of the route chosen. At the same time, there is often a demand to communicate with media. Whether it's a soundbite or a detailed interview, this is a delicate and subtle venture, where overstatement of any kind may endanger what has been achieved.

The negotiator should regard any media appearance as an integral part of the negotiation. Media appearances at times of heightened tension are rarely neutral in end result. They can move the thing along and reinforce it, or they can endanger it. I have seen men who have worked through incredibly difficult negotiations blow the achievement because they couldn't refrain from giving themselves a public pat on the back or resist the temptation to get in a final 'dig'. Protecting what has been achieved is the priority. Everything else is secondary.

I would go further. Where, for example, a large organisation has many regional outposts, I would regard it as a priority to ensure the managers in all of those branch offices are clear on the terms and have a shared interpretation for presentation through local media. Media runs on the exceptional, not on the routine. Accordingly, one local manager who takes a dim view of the announcement as interpreted on the TV news may turn up in the following day's paper as an unnamed source within the organisation, making remarks critical of and perhaps damaging to the results of the negotiation.

In the United States, in cases where a political negotiation has been successfully concluded they go one step further. They brief what they call the 'quote sluts'. These are nationally eminent figures with a known credibility on a particular topic which makes it likely that media will call on them for a reaction to whatever has been accomplished.

The 'quote slut' is made to feel that they are on the inside track by being telephoned with the end result of the negotiation before it enters the public domain, and often assisted – in the case of the publication of complicated documents – by a suggestion that perhaps the most significant emerging change could be found in the second paragraph of page 53.

It's all part of protecting the successful negotiation – the aspect of the negotiation process most under-valued and disregarded by negotiators.

PROTECTING THE AGREEMENT BEGINS WITH THE NEGOTIATION

The ultimate protection of the agreement is the precision which emerges from the discussions. This brings us back to the actual role of clarifying and summarising that happens throughout the whole process. You cannot protect what is not clearly understood by both sides.

LEARNING FROM EACH NEGOTIATION

As soon as a negotiation is completed, at work, at home or socially, we know how we performed. The strongest memory for most people are the things we failed to achieve. Immediately, we make comments such as:

'What I should have said was ... '

'Now I know what I should have done there ... '

Very quickly we move on to another negotiation with no real applied learning from the last one. If it went badly, merciful amnesia comes to our rescue. Ironically, we take away even less from a successful transaction, in that we have no clear idea why there was a beneficial outcome from the negotiation.

You must look back at each negotiation and ask yourself questions like the following:

Did the outcome emerge along the lines that you planned and prepared for? Or was it vastly different from what you predicted? Why the change? Can you trace the point of deviation and the reasons for it?

Write down the outcomes aligned with what you had prepared for:

Had you fully understood what the real interests of the other party were? Did you come up with options that were accepted or formed the basis of the final agreement?

Write down the additional options offered by the other party.

Throughout the discussions were you able to concentrate on the issues and bypass any emotional or personal agendas?

Jot down any potentially provocative statements made.

How far did you help the discussions towards a successful outcome by producing appropriate data or by resorting to objective criteria? What overall lessons did you learn for the future on the four imperatives of negotiation?

Write down the answers to these questions and have them near you when you are planning for your next negotiation. Include observations about advance communication, location, and other practical problems which influenced the negotiation.

TAKEAWAYS

1 Document precisely what has been agreed.
2 Send a written outline of what was agreed and other outcomes.
3 Agree on what is to be communicated to the uninvolved.
4 Remember that media statements or interviews are part of the negotiation process.
5 Precision serves both sides.

9

GIVING FEEDBACK IN NEGOTIATIONS

Inside companies, one of the most difficult negotiations is giving and receiving feedback. Having, down
through the years, studied performance appraisal
systems operating in many companies and organisations, I believe the majority are a waste of time, except
as meeting nominal legal or personal requirements.

The managers who carry out the appraisals don't
like them – in fact they regularly postpone them way
beyond the suggested time-frames. The people who
receive appraisals dread them and derive little or no
benefit from them. They tend to be either euphemistic
and duplicitous or negative, backward-focused fault-
finding. Yet all of us need feedback. Without feedback
there is no learning.

At work everybody needs information about their
performance that will allow them to develop and
change. Not only do they need it but if it is correctly
given they will welcome it. So for starters, I believe we
should speak not about appraisals but about performance review and development negotiation.

Why then do I suggest that it is worthwhile to include feedback or performance review under the term 'negotiation'?

To achieve results that benefit both sides, managers should talk about performance development reviews and should have agreed a personal development programme with each staff member. The review would feed into this programme, so that the context would be one of company investment in the development of people, rather than a punitive annual version of the Leaving Cert, as is – too often – currently the case with this most flawed and unproductive in-company communication.

The exceptions to the rule of flawed negotiation systems are so rare as to be shining examples. The larger and more multinational the company, the greater the level of sophistication but not the level of productive interaction.

Gillian Bowler, who, in addition to running Budget Travel, serves as a non-executive director on a number of company boards, tells a story about a human resources manager in one company who hits a speed bump every time he has to give negative feedback to staff.

'The classic example was a staffer who just wasn't hacking it,' Gillian says. 'This guy just didn't have a great future with the company, because he was mediocre.'

Clear cut situation. Requirement: straight talking. The company wasn't going to sack this executive. They weren't going to make him redundant. But they were going to move him around from job to job, always at the same level, never moving upwards.

In due course, the annual review comes around. Golden opportunity for the HR guy to be straightforward, to help the executive to cop on that – within this particular company – his career path is going nowhere.

After the session is over, the HR guy is asked how it went.

He says, 'Oh, I don't think he's in any doubt about the situation.' End of story, you might think.

But the chief executive of this particular company knows damn well that his HR guy is so nice he's incapable of saying a bad word to anybody.

Knowing that, the CEO asks another question. 'What did you actually say?'

And the HR guy responds, 'Well, I told him he's really going to have to mark out a patch for himself that is his and his alone.'

Oh. Right.

That's telling the guy he has no future in the company?

The guy probably walked away from that and said 'Whoopee, that was a great annual review I just had. Wow, I'm being given specific opportunities here and all I have to do is work out what they should be. Management really think a lot of me.'

According to Gillian Bowler, that approach is a recipe for disappointed expectations, for mistrust, for confusion, for bitterness, and it happens too often in Irish business. She maintains that we're poor at giving feedback because we cannot bear not to be liked. So we soften direct messages and mislead people. Unfortunately people are willing to be misled. They believe what they want to believe.

Or as Francis Bacon observed a few centuries ago: 'What a man had rather were true, he readily believes.'

Essentially that approach to feedback mirrors what I maintained was the wimp approach to negotiations.

There are other managers who demotivate staff by adopting the macho approach to appraisals. Here are some of the statements managers have made to subordinates in appraisal sessions:

- 'You have a truculent attitude and you better change.'
- 'You lack motivation – I want to see you do something about it.'
- 'I get the impression that you just don't care as much about standards as you should. You better start caring.'

Not only do the statements reflect a macho approach to communications, they run counter to the four imperatives for effective negotiation.

- Concentrate on interests and concerns
- Develop options for mutual gain

- Focus on issues (in this case behaviours) not people
- Resort to data and objective criteria

There's another reason for managers to apply the same principles to feedback.

In a court of law – and remember, an appraisal that goes seriously sour can end up in the judicial process – none of these statements quoted alone would stand up. Responses like 'Says who?' and 'Prove it' spring to mind.

Could the HR manager prove someone had a truculent attitude? Possibly.

Let's say the allegedly truculent employee:

- On 16 June arrived an hour late for work, and when asked for an explanation simply shrugged and refused to answer.
- On 2 July gave a response to the auditors consisting of a four letter refusal when they asked a question about inventory levels.
- On 19 July was described by a health and safety inspector as 'singularly unhelpful' when delegated to accompany the HSA officer around the plant.

In that situation, each of the instances might be presented to the employee at the appraisal session, and it would be quite legitimate for the manager to indicate that while, singly, none of these instances are major derogations from duty, collectively, they add up to something serious and negative. However, the proper thing to do is instance the behaviours, if necessary to point out where those behaviours diverge from any articulated company standards, and indicate that there should be no repetition.

In similar vein, if a manager sincerely believes that an employee has lost motivation, that assertion on its own should never be made. Instead, in advance of this most sensitive negotiation, the manager should sit down and so some self-challenging: 'Demotivated is my impression. But impressions are always based on something observed. What is it that I've seen that makes me believe this person is demotivated?'

One manager, challenged on this, said she would need a week to think about it. After the week, she came back with this supportive data about the staff member:

- Sick days (not requiring a sick cert) had doubled in the year in question.
- The staff member had not invested in any new wardrobe and was markedly less well presented than in previous years.
- Two opportunities for promotion had come up – she had applied for neither.

Did this, she asked, not add up to a clear picture of demotivation? The answer is yes.

But it could equally add up to a picture of depression, alcoholism, gambling, loss of personal confidence due to an external factor, tiredness due to taking care of a sick family member or a decision to run regular marathons: the evidence does not point exclusively in one direction.

In such a case, the manager needs to be very careful. If the staff member is within the acceptable number of uncertified sick days, that should not be mentioned at all; the manager is not entitled to draw conclusions from the use of an entitlement. If the lack of a new wardrobe is untypical of the person but if the appearance is acceptable, then the manager again should think twice about raising it; perhaps the staff member can invest heavily in a new wardrobe only once every two years rather than once a year.

Finally, the failure to go for promotion could be interpreted as over- rather than undermotivation: if the staffer wants to stay where she is, then she may lack ambition, but that does not equate to lack of motivation to deliver on the specifications of her present job. A manager may express concern, but if the performance has been up to specification, the manager has no right to make a judgement against an employee based on something as subjective as attributed lack of motivation.

Feedback on Behaviours, Not Attitudes

In an appraisal, there should be specific instances of the behaviours which do not match what is expected. If necessary, several instances may be given to illustrate the cumulative effect, and a clear alternative sought:

> If you check your diary, you'll find, last month, that you were late for four separate meetings. On the last two occasions, I called you on this afterwards

and indicated that this company relies on its staff to be punctual when dealing with clients. Everybody will occasionally fail to meet company standards on a particular issue, but I want to stress this one to you and ask you to make sure that in the coming quarter, you're always at meeting with clients on time or early.

Note the order:

1 Behaviour (specifics and numbers)
2 Statement of company standards
3 Concession that in real life, mistakes are made
4 Iteration of required change

Note, also, what's not in the sequence:

1 No emotion
2 No attribution of motive

Now, even the best feedback is sometimes misunderstood by the recipient, because the whole procedure may have a certain level of tension built into it. There are two ways to obviate misunderstanding of this kind.

The first is to ask for feedback on the feedback. This is where the manager asks the staff member to revise out loud the key points that have been dealt with, and any agreed action arising. The second method is where the manager brings a typed note of the key points to be made, makes them, and both parties sign the notes as a faithful summary of what happened at the meeting. This can then go on file and ensures that both parties approach the following period of time starting from the same base.

If appraisal is used as it should be used, to serve both the development of the individual being appraised and as a management information device, these sessions, ideally, should happen every six months, rather than once a year, to reinforce improvements and monitor any training required.

The final part of any appraisal (Performance Development Review) session should bring the focus to what needs to happen in the future and not concentrate solely on aspects of non-performance in the past. Ongoing feedback on performance should focus on the issues agreed at the formal reviews. There should be no changing of the goalposts.

Positive Reinforcement

Of course, in any company, much feedback goes on, formally or informally, throughout the year, quite apart from the session or sessions devoted to performance appraisal. And although some of that feedback may be characterised by the managerial wish to let someone down easily, it may also take a quite different turn.

Consulting with one company recently, I was questioning a divisional manager who told me, with some pride, that he was a 'firm but fair' manager of people and that he always spoke his mind. As he took a breath, I said that my experience was that whenever someone claimed to always speak their mind, in point of fact, they always spoke their negative mind.

'Can you give me examples where you spoke your positive mind, during the last month?' I asked.

After some thought, he admitted that he could bring to mind no example.

'Speaking your mind is fine,' I suggested, 'As long as the mind is rich in positives and negatives. But if you pride yourself on always calling it as it is, and perceive it to be always negative, then the habit makes you feel better and makes all around you feel worse. Nor does it improve performance, because it militates against the open, two-way communication essential to the delivery and reception of feedback.'

He looked stricken, and commented that he wasn't much for flattery.

'I'm not saying you should flatter your people,' I said. 'On the contrary, the thump on the back, "you're doin' a great job" kind of non-specific praise doesn't work at all in this country, whatever about elsewhere. All of the surveys conducted in companies by Carr Communications indicate that workers want direct, constructive information from managers. They just don't want to be fire-bombed.

TIPS ON GIVING NEGATIVE FEEDBACK

Remember that, however we attempt to couch the reality or the delivery, people hear negative feedback as a put-down or as an attack. So they respond by getting upset, defensive or angry. People will defend themselves against attack but they will let information through. With that in mind:

- Choose the right time and place for feedback
- Alert the other person in advance to the venue and time and ask them to review their own performance in preparation
- Base performance reviews on performance agreements.
- Don't spring issues on staff or examine performance on attributes or behaviours that they didn't know were part of the review
- Give feedback only on specific observed behaviours, not attitudes
- Adopt an **abc** approach to negative feedback:
  What you discuss should be stretching but *achievable*
  Point out how the changes required will *benefit* the staff
  Talk about (and later demonstrate) the *continuing relationship*
- Give time for reaction, reflection and further discussion

For most staff, negative feedback can convey the idea that they have no real future relationship with this manager or this company. The manager must demonstrate after the review that nothing has changed. This is part of protecting the outcome. Ask the staff member as soon as possible to undertake a responsible task. This demonstrates no change in the relationship. In other words, as in classical negotiation, separate people from the problem. Don't label people. Talk about what the person does, not what they are or you think they are.

TAKEAWAYS

1 Correctly given, feedback on performance is welcomed.

2 Apply the imperatives of negotiation to feedback on work performance.

3 Be clear – don't cloud the message by adopting the wimp approach.

4 Be careful – the macho approach to feedback is counter-productive.

5 Collect observable behaviour evidence.

6 Don't given feedback on attitudes. Employers buy behaviour and activities. Totalitarian rulers want to own attitudes too.

7 Focus on the future, not just on non-performance in the past.

8 Multiply the occasions of positive reinforcement.

9 Show by your behaviour that the feedback session has not changed the day-to-day working relationship.